THE
CONVENTION
PROBLEM

Studies in Presidential Selection
TITLES PUBLISHED

Voting for President
WALLACE S. SAYRE *and* JUDITH H. PARRIS

Financing Presidential Campaigns
DELMER D. DUNN

The Convention Problem
JUDITH H. PARRIS

☆
Judith H. Parris
☆

THE
CONVENTION
PROBLEM

Issues in Reform of
Presidential Nominating Procedures

Studies in Presidential Selection
THE BROOKINGS INSTITUTION
Washington, D.C.

Library of Congress Cataloging in Publication Data:
Parris, Judith H
   The convention problem.
   (Studies in presidential selection)
   Bibliography: p.
   1. Political conventions.   2. Nominations for
office—U.S.   3. Presidents—U.S.—Election.
I. Title.   II. Series.
JK2255.P35   324'.21'0973   72-143
ISBN 0-8157-6928-8
ISBN 0-8157-6927-x (pbk.)

THE BROOKINGS INSTITUTION is an independent organization devoted to nonpartisan research, education, and publication in economics, government, foreign policy, and the social sciences generally. Its principal purposes are to aid in the development of sound public policies and to promote public understanding of issues of national importance.

The Institution was founded on December 8, 1927, to merge the activities of the Institute for Government Research, founded in 1916, the Institute of Economics, founded in 1922, and the Robert Brookings Graduate School of Economics and Government, founded in 1924.

The general administration of the Institution is the responsibility of a Board of Trustees charged with maintaining the independence of the staff and fostering the most favorable conditions for creative research and education. The immediate direction of the policies, program, and staff of the Institution is vested in the President, assisted by an advisory committee of the officers and staff.

In publishing a study, the Institution presents it as a competent treatment of a subject worthy of public consideration. The interpretations and conclusions in such publications are those of the author or authors and do not necessarily reflect the views of the other staff members, officers, or trustees of the Brookings Institution.

FOREWORD

ALTHOUGH it has been the established system for nominating presidential candidates for more than a century, the national party convention has been the object of persistent criticism from those who have considered it an inappropriate mechanism for deciding who has a real chance to become President of the United States. The criticism was intensified after the unseemly events that seemed to dominate the 1964 Republican and 1968 Democratic conventions. Further underscoring the widespread public concern about conventions is a contemporary trend toward closer scrutiny of many public institutions, from giant corporations to the family unit.

The analysis in this book deals with critical issues in the reform of the presidential nominating convention: apportionment, delegate selection, convention management, platform writing, and the role of the media. The issues are examined against a background question that asks to what extent a political convention can be termed "fair" and "democratic." The era of the nationally televised convention—the period beginning in 1952—is the focus of attention. While sympathetic to the intentions of reformers, the author assesses the clash of their objectives with the traditional purposes of conventions aimed at quickly selecting a presidential ticket that will be victorious in the ensuing election.

Judith H. Parris is a Research Associate in the Brookings Governmental Studies Program. This book is one of a series of studies in presidential selection undertaken by the Governmental Studies Program under the direction of Gilbert Y. Steiner. These studies follow earlier Brookings research that in 1960 produced *The Politics of National Party Conventions*, by Paul T. David, Ralph M. Goldman, and Richard C. Bain, as well as a number of subsequent volumes. Earlier books in the current series include *Voting for President: The Electoral College and the American Political System*, by Wallace S. Sayre and Judith H. Parris, and *Financing Presidential Campaigns*, by Delmer D. Dunn. The present study and additional work in progress has been carried out under the general supervision of Donald R. Matthews.

A bipartisan public advisory council, whose members are listed in the front of this book, offers practical comment and assistance for the series of studies in presidential selection. Additional assistance on this book has been provided by a small group of scholars who met at Brookings in October 1971 to discuss their reactions to an earlier draft; their suggestions are acknowledged with thanks and have been taken into account in subsequent revisions. Participants in the conference are listed at the end of this volume. The author also wishes to acknowledge the receipt of particularly useful information and observations from Thomas E. Cronin, Paul T. David, Delmer D. Dunn, William J. Gammie, Howard G. Gamser, Josephine Good, Bryce Harlow, William R. Keech, Gladys E. Lang, Charles McDowell, Jr., Daniel A. Mazmanian, and Robert W. Nelson. Virginia C. Haaga edited the manuscript and Joan C. Culver prepared the index. Sara Sklar handled secretarial duties with admirable dispatch and with assistance from Margie Barringer and Michele Larrere.

Financial support for the project of which this book is a part was provided by a grant from the Ford Foundation. The views, opinions, and interpretations in this book are those of the author and do not necessarily represent the views of the other staff members, officers, or trustees of the Brookings Institution or of the Ford Foundation.

KERMIT GORDON
President

January 1972
Washington, D.C.

CONTENTS

Foreword vii

I. THE NEW DEBATE ABOUT CONVENTIONS   I

Conventions: Why and How 3
Perennial Dissatisfaction 6
The New Debate 8
Criteria for Evaluating Conventions 12

II. APPORTIONING THE VOTES   16

The 1912 Republican Convention 17
Recent Law Suits 18
The Republican Party 21
The Democratic Party 27
Alternative Plans for Allocating Votes 36

III. SELECTING THE DELEGATES   51

Institutions for Selecting Delegates 52
Characteristics of the Delegates 58
Credentials Contests 62
Alternative Standards for Delegate Selection 68

IV. FAIRNESS, DEMOCRACY, AND DELIBERATION   81

The Character of Convention Deliberation 81
Size and Deliberation 86
Procedural Rules and Deliberation 96
Beyond the Rules 106

V. WRITING THE PLATFORM   109

The Significance of Platforms 109
Drafting the Platforms 114
Alternatives 130

VI. THE PRESS, THE PUBLIC, AND THE POLITICIANS   142

   The Press and the Public 143
   The Impact on Conventions 149
   The Press and the Politicians 153
   Issues and Alternatives 158

VII. SOLUTIONS   172

   The Primary Alternative 172
   Toward Fair and Democratic Conventions 177
   Solving the Convention Problem 180

   CONFERENCE PARTICIPANTS   181

   SELECTED BIBLIOGRAPHY   183

   INDEX   189

   TABLES

2-1. *Apportionment of Votes at the 1972 Republican National Convention*   24
2-2. *Voting Strength of Selected Groups of States, as a Percentage of Total, at Republican National Conventions, 1952–72*   27
2-3. *Apportionment of Votes at the 1972 Democratic National Convention*   32
2-4. *Voting Strength of Selected Groups of States, as a Percentage of Total, at Democratic National Conventions, 1952–72*   34
2-5. *Voting Strength of the States at the 1972 Republican National Convention under Various Apportionment Formulas*   44
2-6. *Voting Strength of the States at the 1972 Democratic National Convention under Various Apportionment Formulas*   46
2-7. *Voting Strength of Selected Groups of States, as a Percentage of Total, at the 1972 Republican Convention, under Various Apportionment Formulas*   48
2-8. *Voting Strength of Selected Groups of States, as a Percentage of Total, at the 1972 Democratic Convention, under Various Apportionment Formulas*   48
3-1. *Delegate Selection Methods Used in 1968*   52
3-2. *Characteristics of Delegates to the 1968 Democratic and Republican Conventions*   59
3-3. *Characteristics of Total Population of the United States and of Persons Eligible to Vote, 1968*   60
3-4. *Characteristics of Presidential Voters, 1968: Percentage of Each Category Voting for the Democratic and Republican Tickets*   61
4-1. *Numbers of Delegates and Alternates at the Major Party National Conventions, 1952–68*   87

Contents   xi

5-1. *Content of Democratic and Republican Party Platforms, 1952–68*   111
5-2. *The Fulfillment of Testable Major Party Platform Pledges, 1944–66*   113
6-1. *Medium That Would Be Believed in Case of Conflicting*
     Reports, 1959–68   146
6-2. *Number of Sessions and Duration of the Major Party National*
     Conventions, 1952–68   150

THE
CONVENTION
PROBLEM

☆

Chapter One

☆

THE NEW DEBATE ABOUT CONVENTIONS

*Discontent is the first step in the progress
of a man or a nation.*
Oscar Wilde

THERE ARE MANY possible ways of selecting a national party
leader. When formal political parties were first instituted in the
United States early in the nineteenth century, presidential candidates were nominated by the party's congressional caucus. In
Great Britain's parliamentary system of government, the party's
leader still is chosen by the legislative elders. This system has its
advantages: the party's national legislators presumably are well
acquainted with the qualifications of the candidates, have the
party's interests at heart, and are good judges of vote-getting ability. But in the United States the caucus system suffered in 1824
when the candidate chosen by this method finished third in a four-
man race. Moreover, the idea of selection by an elite group of
leaders collided with the mood of frontier democracy symbolized
by Andrew Jackson. Jackson's election in 1828 marked the end
of the caucus system. Since 1832, all major candidates have been
nominated by national conventions.[1]

1. The definitive work on convention processes has been done by Paul T. David
and his associates. See Paul T. David, Ralph M. Goldman, and Richard C. Bain, *The
Politics of National Party Conventions* (Brookings Institution, 1960); Paul T. David,
Malcolm Moos, and Ralph M. Goldman, *Presidential Nominating Politics in 1952*, 5
vols. (Johns Hopkins Press, 1954); and Richard C. Bain, *Convention Decisions and
Voting Records* (Brookings Institution, 1960).

The presidential nominating convention today is a quasi-legal body governed by rules established by the parties themselves.[2] Traditionally it has carried out four functions: it has nominated candidates, drafted the party platform, governed the party (through the national committee between conventions), and rallied the faithful to begin the campaign. When the convention works well, it is, as its name would imply, a "coming together." It is an occasion for forming a consensus that will unite the party and impel it toward victory. In modern times it also serves to legitimate the choice of a presidential nominee that usually is determined for all practical purposes in polls and primaries before the convention opens.

When a party is as bitterly divided, however, as the Republicans were in 1964 and the Democrats in 1968, the convention works less well in achieving consensus and legitimation. "After Carl Albert adjourned the 1968 Democratic National Convention . . . ," a sympathetic observer has written, "a good many Democrats . . . left Chicago's tear-gassed streets and stink-bombed hotels convinced that something was terribly wrong with the traditional way the party had gone about choosing its presidential nominee."[3] Four years earlier in San Francisco, after a convention that was "not a meeting, not a clash, but a *coup d'état*,"[4] many Republicans who survived its emotional frenzy had been equally disillusioned.

The structure and operations of national conventions have received more critical public attention during the past few years than at any other time in their history. Yet only a few people deeply concerned with politics fully understand arcane arguments about methods of apportioning votes, or delegate selection sys-

2. State laws specify the procedures to be used if delegates are selected in primary elections or, as in many states, in conventions; and constitutional guarantees have been construed to prohibit discrimination against Negroes and other groups in party processes.

3. Austin Ranney, "Turnout and Representation in Presidential Primary Elections," paper delivered at the annual meeting of the American Political Science Association, Sept. 7–11, 1971, p. 1.

4. Theodore H. White, *The Making of the President 1964* (Atheneum, 1965), p. 202.

tems, or parliamentary procedures. The purpose of this book is to clarify the debate and to set forth the political implications of various possible changes in party conventions.

The significance of the current debate over convention reform is considerable. While neither omniscient nor omnipotent, the President is the most important single figure in U.S. politics.[5] The Democratic and Republican conventions are the formal arenas where the range of presidential candidates with a chance of winning is narrowed from perhaps dozens to two. This is one of the most decisive choices in the nation's politics, sometimes more important than the November election. Amending the ground rules of convention contests might mean changing the constituency of the presidential nominee. Such a change, in turn, would affect who was nominated, who was elected, and what the person who captured the presidency could and could not do once in office.

Although it is rarely discussed explicitly, the underlying issue of the debate is what role the national convention as an institution should play. Should it be a representative assembly, or a deliberative body, or both? If the first, then whom should it represent? Who should constitute the national party that convenes every four years—elected party officials, long-time party workers, recent enthusiasts, party voters, registered partisans, or a broader constituency? How should the unit of representation be determined, how should the representatives be selected, and how should they be linked to their constituents? In deliberation, who should take part in which decisions and in what ways?

Conventions: Why and How

The national convention is a unique institution. Whereas most political institutions and the governing bodies of most private or-

5. For a revisionist view of presidential power, see Thomas E. Cronin, "The Textbook Presidency and Political Science," paper delivered at the annual meeting of the American Political Science Association, Los Angeles, September 7–12, 1970. An abridged version was published in *The Washington Monthly*, Vol. 2 (October 1970), pp. 47–54.

ganizations are composed overwhelmingly of persons with long tenure and consequent familiarity with the rules of conducting the institution's business, conventions frequently have a sizable segment of insurgent delegations and others with little or no previous national convention experience.[6] The lifetime of conventions is also much shorter than that of many other assemblies. For bodies whose decisions are of profound national and even international significance, the conventions perform their business with considerable dispatch. In most respects, presidential nominating conventions more nearly resemble union conventions, trade and professional association annual meetings, and stockholders' meetings than other political conclaves. They differ from comparable private gatherings mainly in their far greater degree of genuine competition over the selection of leaders, policy recommendations, and other issues. Finally, no other representative institution receives such scrutiny from the news media; even the U.S. Congress, covered daily by scores of journalists, does not permit television reporters and cameras to broadcast proceedings from the House and Senate floors.

Because of these characteristics, the atmosphere of presidential nominating conventions is unique. Several thousand people, most of them parochial in outlook and strangers to one another, are thrown together for a few days to make a set of major decisions under conditions of great strain and maximum publicity. Arthur M. Schlesinger, Jr., has captured the convention spirit:

> American politics has an occasion to match every mood: ceremony, circus, farce, melodrama, tragedy. Nothing rolls them together more opulently than a presidential convention; nothing else offers all at once the whirl, the excitement, the gaiety, the intrigue and the anguish. But a convention is far too fluid and hysterical a phenomenon for exact history. Everything happens at once and everywhere, and everything changes too quickly. People talk too much, smoke too much, rush too much and sleep too little. Fatigue tightens nerves and produces a sus-

6. See John W. Soule and James W. Clarke, "Amateurs and Professionals: A Study of Delegates to the 1968 Democratic National Convention," *American Political Science Review*, Vol. 64 (September 1970), pp. 888–98.

ceptibility to rumor and panic. . . . At the time it is all a confusion; in retrospect it is all a blur.[7]

Conventions appear to be "all a confusion" because in fact they are made up of many groups of quite purposeful people doing many different things, sometimes simultaneously. What they do depends largely on the strategic context. The most important factor is whether the party is in or out of power. The party out of power divides its loyalties among various aspirants for the presidential nomination and other national spokesmen. The central focus of the party in power is the White House, particularly when the President seeks to stay in office. When the incumbent is retiring, the heir apparent and any other candidates are autonomous power centers.

In the case of the party in power, the President, his staff, and other confidants seek to protect his interests: his personal prestige and popularity, his policies and programs, and his preferences about the party future. They want to maintain—and project the image of—a party united behind the President. If he seeks to succeed himself, of course, the nomination is their primary goal; even if he does not, however, they try to keep his stamp on the national party. The presidential group has allies throughout the convention organization. The national chairman is the President's choice; and the convention officers and officials, committee chairmen, and national committee staff—all named by the national chairman— reflect his inclinations.

When the party does not have an incumbent President seeking its nomination (or if his nomination is contested), the various candidates for the office and their organizations actively pursue delegate votes. Press secretaries woo the news media in the hope of influencing the voters through them. Friends of the candidates also work to obtain a platform acceptable to their faction. Other associates may try to change various convention rules in the in-

---

7. Arthur M. Schlesinger, Jr., *A Thousand Days: John F. Kennedy in the White House* (Houghton Mifflin, 1965), p. 33.

terest of their candidate, as the Eisenhower forces did in 1952 and
McCarthy supporters sought to do in 1968.

Meanwhile, at all conventions a variety of other persons are
performing other tasks. The planners, managers, and operatives
of the conclave aim at putting on a show that will work smoothly,
satisfy party leaders, unify the faithful, and win votes in November—objectives that frequently conflict with one another, especially at conventions where the presidential nomination is contested. Simultaneously, the convention committees on the platform,
credentials, rules, and (in the Republican party) permanent organization are carrying on their deliberations—not without regard
for the strategic context of their efforts. The state delegations
are caucusing and organizing themselves formally as well as into
factional groups based on candidate preferences, policy views,
and other issues. Many individual delegates, particularly some in
large delegations who are not committee members or leaders in
any convention group, are busy wondering what they are supposed
to be doing. Representatives of the news media are seeking to get
stories by interviewing candidates, party leaders, campaign managers, delegates, and anyone else who can provide useful material
about the convention. Spokesmen for various interest groups are
buttonholing anyone they think can help them promote their
candidate, platform proposals, or other objectives.

Perennial Dissatisfaction

Criticism of this quadrennial series of activities is not new.
Writing at the turn of the century, the Russian scholar Ostrogorski called the national convention "a colossal travesty of popular institutions."[8] For H. L. Mencken, in 1932 it was a "colossal
clown show."[9] They agreed at least on the magnitude of the
problem.

8. M. Ostrogorski, *Democracy and the Organization of Political Parties*, Vol. 2, *The United States*, edited and abridged by Seymour Martin Lipset (Quadrangle Books, 1964), p. 143.
9. H. L. Mencken, *Making a President* (Knopf, 1932), p. 31.

There have been three specific indictments of national conventions since they began during the 1830s. The boldest has been the assertion by the Progressives that conventions are inherently undemocratic. Candidate selection, in the Progressive view, can be democratic only when it is carried out directly by the voters in primary elections. In nominations for lesser offices in the United States, the convention largely has been abandoned in favor of the direct primary. Since the Progressive heyday during the early twentieth century, however, many political scientists and politicians have had second thoughts about the universal desirability of primaries. They have pointed out that voters may not always be well informed about all the candidates, particularly those seeking minor offices; that primary voters as a group may differ significantly from the total population and from party members as a group;[10] and that when there are more than two candidates for a single office, a primary may be a less satisfactory method—and is no more democratic a method—than the bargaining processes of a convention. A single primary measures the first preferences of those who vote; it does not build a party consensus behind a single standard-bearer. And a primary with a runoff election between the top two candidates is excessively costly for all concerned. Indeed, any nationwide system of presidential primaries in lieu of a convention would entail tremendous outlays of money and excruciating physical and emotional wear and tear on the candidates.

Less fundamental but important is the criticism that conventions are undignified forums for selecting the nation's top leaders. Former President Eisenhower told the Republican National Committee that the party's discordant 1964 convention was "a disgrace"[11] and recommended changes in arrangements and organizational procedures aimed at making the convention a more

10. See Ranney, "Turnout and Representation in Presidential Primary Elections." But statewide experience, reported by Ranney, is not necessarily applicable to a national primary.

11. His criticisms were subsequently published in Dwight D. Eisenhower, "Our National Nominating Conventions Are a Disgrace," *Reader's Digest*, Vol. 89 (July 1966), pp. 76–80.

seemly mechanism for nominating candidates for the highest office in the land. Complaints of this order persist, although some historians believe that contemporary excesses of partisan exuberance are fewer and less extreme than they were in earlier times.

Another persistent but more trivial criticism is that conventions are dull. Increasingly this has come from observers—the press corps and televiewers—who find many aspects of conventions less than entertaining. Accordingly they recommend shortening the sessions, eliminating activities whose principal objective is to create publicity for minor candidates, and generally improving the quality of the show. Their comments recall the annual post-mortems of telecasts of the motion picture industry's Academy Awards ceremony. The criticism may be valid, but it is certainly of secondary importance.

The New Debate

The new criticism of conventions cuts far deeper. It reflects a current and broader reconsideration of the impact of many major national institutions on the citizenry, and vice versa. In recent years virtually every social institution—the government, the corporation, the church, the school, and even the family—has been minutely examined and reexamined, often found wanting, and sometimes rejected by those examining it. Thus it is hardly surprising that the presidential nominating convention, which is telecast for hours to millions of viewers, has been subjected to renewed scrutiny.

While the new criticism accepts the convention as a legitimate instrument for nominating presidential candidates, it questions the essential fairness and democracy of convention procedures. It argues that they consistently have helped those who are already in control of party organizations and correspondingly have hurt those seeking to obtain such power. In this sense, the criticism is related to a power struggle; but it also has serious implications that transcend immediate political concerns. In particular, it assumes that conventions are at least quasi-public institutions rather than assemblies to be manipulated by an inside group of leaders.

This perspective was dramatized at the 1968 Democratic convention. Although virtually certain that their candidate would not win the presidential nomination, supporters of Minnesota Senator Eugene J. McCarthy, and also some allies backing other candidates, objected to the procedures that were used against them. First they recoiled during the pre-convention campaign from state systems of delegate selection that precluded any timely expression of voter preferences or left McCarthy with proportionately fewer votes than his showing in primaries or state conventions seemed to warrant. As a result, at the national convention the McCarthy forces challenged a record number of delegate credentials. Nearly all the challenges were unsuccessful. Then, as the platform was being considered and the time came for balloting on the presidential nomination, the insurgents charged that the convention leadership was deliberately abridging their rights to full expression of their views and discriminating against their activities in both major and minor ways. Accordingly they stepped up their protests from the convention floor.

The nature and persistence of these protests were highly unusual. For persons who lose political contests to complain in public is understandable but is generally considered bad form. The grounds for the complaints that are voiced are sometimes that the system was structured in favor of the winner. But never before in recent memory of conventions has this criticism been raised to the point of philosophical principle and insisted upon by the losers after the nomination decision has been made. Under the leadership of the then Governor of Iowa, Harold E. Hughes, however, critics at the 1968 Democratic convention produced a lengthy report on the method of selecting presidential nominees. The report concluded that the party's systems of delegate selection and many of its convention procedures, particularly the winner-take-all unit rule of voting, were undemocratic.[12] The thrust of its arguments evidently made a deep and lasting impression; its central concerns with delegate selection methods and the "open convention" have been at the core of the subsequent debate.

In the aftermath of disorder in the hall and violence on the streets of Chicago, party leaders sought to restore what they believed to be waning public confidence in the presidential nominating system. The bitter Democrats united long enough at the convention to abolish the unit rule, under which a majority of the delegates from a state may cast the state's entire vote, regardless of the preference of the minority. At the same time, the delegates passed a resolution guaranteeing that the state parties would do their best to select 1972 convention delegates under procedures open to public participation during calendar year 1972. Under this mandate, the Democratic National Chairman, Senator Fred R. Harris of Oklahoma, subsequently appointed two commissions to implement the reforms: a Commission on Party Structure and Delegate Selection, headed by Senator George S. McGovern of South Dakota (and later by Representative Donald M. Fraser of Minnesota), which dealt with activities of the state and local parties that were related to the national convention; and a Commission on Rules, chaired by Michigan Representative James G. O'Hara, which drafted the first formal regulations ever written for Democratic national conventions. The two Democratic commissions had advantages for both the insurgents and the established leadership that they had opposed. The commissions provided a forum for the discussion of specific grievances and for consideration of reform proposals. They re-established communication between the alienated insurgents and the national committee. As a result they had the potential to help heal the wounds inflicted in 1968 and to prevent the injured from turning their efforts to a minor party movement that could hurt the Democrats in future years.

12. Commission vice chairman Donald M. Fraser inserted its report in the *Congressional Record*. Vol. 114, 90 Cong. 2 sess. (1968), pp. 31544–60.

Politically, the Republican convention situation was unlike that
of the Democrats. The Republicans have adhered very strictly to
an official written code, whereas the Democrats until quite recently have proceeded "on a sort of common-law basis."[13] A
fundamental divergence in political style and temperament may
be the reason. As Anne O'Hare McCormick put it, "To the Republicans, politics is a business, while to the Democrats, it's a
pleasure."[14] Clinton Rossiter observed:

> A gathering of Democrats *is* more sweaty, disorderly, offhand, and
> rowdy than a gathering of Republicans; it is also likely to be more
> cheerful, imaginative, tolerant of dissent, and skillful at the game of
> give-and-take. A gathering of Republicans *is* more respectable, sober,
> purposeful, and businesslike than a gathering of Democrats; it is also
> likely to be more self-righteous, pompous, cut-and-dried, and just
> plain boring.[15]

The difference in political style flows in part from the parties'
makeup. The Democrats are more socially heterogeneous and
willing to disagree publicly; the Republicans are more homogene-
ously middle class and devoted to organization, neatness, and
efficiency.

In addition the Republicans have changed their convention
procedures in recent years. After major credentials fights between
the Taft and Eisenhower forces in 1952 (see Chapter 3), the party
amended its formal rules to (1) prohibit contested delegates from
voting on seating disputes unless the delegates had been supported
by at least two-thirds of the credentials committee; (2) establish
a contests committee within the Republican National Committee
to hold fact-finding hearings in advance of the convention; and
(3) provide ground rules for participation and candidacy in the
delegate selection process. Again, after the 1964 convention and
former President Eisenhower's call for change, the Republican

13. David, Moos, and Goldman, *Presidential Nominating Politics*, p. 85.

14. Quoted in Ralph G. Martin, *Ballots and Bandwagons* (Rand McNally, 1964),
p. 311.

15. Clinton Rossiter, *Parties and Politics in America* (Cornell University Press,
1960), p. 117.

National Committee established a Committee on Convention Reforms that investigated ways of improving order and decorum at the national convention. The reform panel's recommendations provided the basis for a number of procedural changes, including stricter control over access to the delegates' section of the convention floor, use of professional security guards only, and shorter convention sessions with briefer speeches and fewer formal ceremonies.

When public interest in convention operations became evident after the Democrats' unfortunate experience in 1968, the Republicans rose to the challenge of the new criticism. The ability of President Nixon's party to agree was increased by his central direction; this contrasted favorably with the fundamentally leaderless and squabbling Democrats. In accordance with a rule approved by the 1968 convention, the Republican National Chairman appointed a Delegates and Organizations (DO) Committee under the leadership of Rosemary Ginn, the Republican national committeewoman from Missouri, to study the extent of adherence to a new rule forbidding barriers to participation in the delegate selection process that are based on race, religion, color, or national origin.

Since this book was written during a time when the Democrats were making more fundamental changes in their convention, Republicans may charge with some justification that their party has been accorded secondary attention in the pages that follow. Whatever the genesis of suggestions for new departures, however, there is no inherent reason why they are more applicable to Democratic than to Republican conventions. If any standards are to be required of the bodies that nominate presidential candidates, the standards apply equally well to both Republicans and Democrats.

Criteria for Evaluating Conventions

How are conventions to be assessed? In the past, they have usually been *remembered* for dramatic events—speeches, floor fights, or walkouts—but have been *judged* on the basis of their output, particularly the presidential candidates they produced. Many political leaders have sought the nominee who would help their local cause the most. In the aggregate, this has meant that conventions ought to nominate the candidate most capable of winning the election nationwide. In a two-party system only half the conventions actually can succeed in nominating a national winner. But even the party that is unsuccessful in November can do its best to select its potentially strongest vote-getter. Though politicians may quibble about "what-ifs," the conventions almost always have chosen the clear front-runner as the party's nominee, at least since systematic national polling began in 1936. Again, idealistic commentators on conventions have used the test of whether "the best man"—the most qualified, the most experienced, the one with the most appropriate policy views—has been nominated. Many in this school of criticism have remembered James Bryce's point that great men are not chosen President but have forgotten that one of the reasons Bryce offered for this pattern was that great leaders are not always required. In any case the quality of presidents or candidates is not by itself an adequate standard for judging the quality of the process by which they have been selected.

While the new debate about the presidential nominating convention has focused directly on the quality of the procedures for making the choice, many commentators long have accepted a lack of internal democracy in the Democratic and Republican parties as unavoidable, although undesirable. They have argued that while each necessarily was run by small groups of leaders, the important issue was the extent of real and fair competition *between* the parties. This position is less widely accepted today. When only two political parties have a real chance of winning the presidency, every citizen has a legitimate stake in the process by which they select their nominees. Moreover, the new public scrutiny of various national institutions means that criticisms of party operations will be broadcast by the news media and taken seriously by the voters; thus, politicians too must take them seriously.

The general thrust of the new reform movement has been concern with the extent of fairness and democracy—as well as the traditional values of efficiency, reasonableness, consensus, and legitimacy—found in the presidential nominating process. These are elusive values, not easily defined even in the specific issues and instances that have attracted the attention of contemporary reformers.

Generally, however, the quality of *fairness* has meant that the rules of the convention system should not discriminate systematically against any group and that the rules themselves should be applied consistently, regardless of who gains and who loses as a result of their application in a particular instance. Because of the presence of television, conventions must not only *be* fair, they must *look* fair.

Democracy is not often rigorously defined. Indeed, it is more accurate to describe an operating institution as either more or less democratic, rather than ideally so. A party convention, to be acceptably democratic, should have several characteristics. Its votes should be so apportioned as to represent the party's constituents in the electorate on a reasonably equal basis. Its delegates and alternates should represent the views—particularly the candidate preferences—of those constituents insofar as they can be determined. Delegates and alternates should be chosen by the popular vote of party adherents or by state party officials elected for that specific purpose; the candidates who received the most votes should participate in the convention. At the national convention, major decisions should be made by popular vote of the delegates or by committees or officials who were chosen or at least ratified by the delegates and whose actions were subject to the vote of the full convention. In such decision-making, each individual's vote should count equally, and the side with a simple majority of the votes should win.

The contemporary convention problem is that recent demands for fairness and democracy in procedures may clash headlong with the convention's traditional objectives of efficiency, legitimacy, reasonableness, and unity as a means to victory. For example, it may be difficult to reconcile fairness to every faction with the rapid choice of a nominee and approval of a platform and the rallying of a broad party consensus. And a party that bares its internal struggles to public scrutiny may find it difficult to win elections. The new thrust is toward diversity, while the old impulse was toward unity. As a result, the modifications in conventions required by the new values suggest far more extensive change than mere tinkering with the formal structure would seem to imply.

☆

Chapter Two

☆

APPORTIONING THE VOTES

Politics . . . ain't bean bag.
Finley Peter Dunne

SINCE POLITICS is "who gets what, when, how,"[1] the apportionment of voting power is always centrally important in any political institution. The system used for distributing votes determines the relative strength of political factions. Accordingly, politicians have displayed endless fascination with, and arithmetic ingenuity in, devising apportionment formulas.

While all politicians are concerned with who has power and who wins, party reformers have been concerned also with the equity of systems for allocating votes—in state legislatures, in Congress, in the electoral college, and in presidential nominating conventions. Reformers have often concluded that the systems used are undemocratic because they do not provide for equal representation.

But just who is being represented at presidential nominating conventions? Is the convention preeminently a gathering representative of those who support the party at the polls? If so, then partisan voters should be the dominant element in any apportionment scheme. Or is the convention representative of the whole populace? In that case, population is the most equitable basis for allocating votes. Or perhaps a convention is rightly viewed as *both* a partisan and a public institution, and thus both criteria should be taken into account. Again, a convention can be considered as a

---

1. See Harold D. Lasswell, *Politics: Who Gets What, When, How* (McGraw-Hill, 1936).

parley of party leaders, which implies that votes should be apportioned directly to constituent party organizations. Fundamental issues of definition must be resolved in any choice among the various methods of allocating the votes.

These distinctions are not merely academic. In this century arguments over them have shattered one convention and caused the party to lose an election. And they are still of sufficient practical importance to generate lawsuits that go all the way to the Supreme Court.

The 1912 Republican Convention

The classic example of how the apportionment system has actually affected both the convention and the subsequent election is provided by the Republican convention of 1912. In that year, incumbent President William Howard Taft ran for renomination against former Republican President Theodore Roosevelt. Under the convention rules, each state was awarded four delegates at large plus two delegates for each of its congressional districts. This meant that GOP delegates from the then solidly Democratic South were, in the words of William Jennings Bryan, "representing mythical constituencies"[2]—or more precisely, constituencies of many non-voters, predominantly black, and voters the overwhelming majority of whom were Democrats. Apportionment was based on state population and not on state party strength. In over half the congressional districts concerned, the Republicans had not even run candidates for the House in 1910. The convention delegates from these southern areas were mostly professional politicians who lived on patronage supplied them by the White House. Not surprisingly, they supported the renomination of President Taft, who was in the best position to affect their fortunes.

The Roosevelt forces waged a major battle over the credentials of these and other delegations. They contested the seats of 256

2. William Jennings Bryan, *A Tale of Two Conventions* (Funk & Wagnalls, 1912), p. xxi.

delegates, 176 of them from the eleven states of the old Confederacy. The Republican National Committee, composed predominantly of Taft loyalists, duly heard the complaints and recommended to the convention that Taft be given 235 of the contested seats. Under then-existing party rules, the challenged delegates themselves were permitted to vote on the credentials cases. On the first decisive roll call the Taft forces won, 558 to 501. The margin of victory was provided by the contested southern delegates.[3]

Still, the Roosevelt partisans did not capitulate without a struggle:

> During the nominating and seconding speeches, the galleries screamed insults and curses at the Taft men, most of whom screamed right back. The aisles were jammed with shouting, struggling delegates, and the cry of "steamroller" echoed through the audience.[4]

When it was clear that his side had lost, Roosevelt urged his delegates not to vote when the roll was called. His ultimate recourse was the Progressive party, and his candidacy on that ticket in November helped the Democrats to win the presidency for the first time in twenty years.

Recent Law Suits

Apportionment has been a bone of contention in more recent times. On January 10, 1972, the United States Supreme Court refused without comment to review a Court of Appeals ruling reversing a district court decision that had struck down the apportionment formula of the Democratic National Committee for the 1972 convention. The formula allocated 54 percent of the convention votes to the states on the basis of strength in the electoral college (equal to a state's total number of United States

3. See Paul T. David, Ralph M. Goldman, and Richard C. Bain, *The Politics of National Party Conventions* (Brookings Institution, 1960), p. 167; and Eugene H. Roseboom, *A History of Presidential Elections from George Washington to Richard M. Nixon*, 3rd ed. (Macmillan, 1970), pp. 362–63.
4. Herbert Eaton, *Presidential Timber* (Free Press, 1964), p. 220.

senators and representatives) and 46 percent on the basis of the average Democratic vote for President in each state in the three preceding elections. The district court had termed the national committee's formula discriminatory, lacking in rational basis, and unconstitutional, and had ordered the national committee to use a new apportionment method based simply on the number of voters in each state who had voted Democratic in one or more preceding presidential elections. The court of appeals in reversing the decision said that basing apportionment on Democratic voting for President alone was too rigid and went beyond the guarantees implied by the Fourteenth Amendment.

The decisions came in a suit filed against the national Democratic party by Kenneth A. Bode, director of the Center for Political Reform (a private organization established to monitor the Democrats' commissions on rules and party structure and delegate selection); by the Democratic national committeemen, national committeewomen, and state chairmen from New York and California; by the head of the Americans for Democratic Action; and by other prominent liberal Democrats. Essentially they argued that the convention strength of some states and their voters, including New York and California, was unfairly diluted by the Democratic National Committee's apportionment scheme because it deviated from what they called a one-Democrat-one-vote standard. The plaintiffs sought a new apportionment formula based wholly on each state's percentage of the Democratic popular vote in the immediately preceding presidential election or elections.

Meanwhile, a group of Democrats at the opposite end of the party spectrum had sued their party, and the Republicans as well, on completely different grounds. Georgia Attorney General Arthur K. Bolton in 1970 filed suit on behalf of his state in the United States District Court for the District of Columbia, charging that Georgia citizens would be denied equal rights in the 1972 conventions because the Democratic and Republican parties deviated from the one-person-one-vote standard in their convention apportionment formulas. The complaint, signed by then-Governor

Lester G. Maddox and other state officials and citizens, named as defendants the national Democratic party, the national Republican party, the two national committees, and the national committeemen and committeewomen of each party for the District of Columbia.

The plaintiffs' petition argued that Georgia would be at a disadvantage compared to some other states at the 1972 conventions because both the Democrats and the Republicans for many years have awarded extra convention votes to states that the party's presidential ticket had carried in the previous election. Georgia in 1972 would not be eligible for these bonus votes in either party because it had supported George Wallace in 1968. The Georgia plaintiffs contended that they were being unfairly discriminated against by this system—that their state would not receive the share of Democratic and Republican convention votes to which it was rightly entitled by its population.[5] The District court rejected the suit on procedural grounds. When the plaintiffs appealed, the Court of Appeals also ruled against them, holding that population alone was an inappropriate basis for convention apportionment since only part of the populace adheres to a single party. The Supreme Court denied the Georgians' petition for certiorari.

The principal irony of the Georgia suit was, of course, that the one-person-one-vote standard had originated in Supreme Court rulings that Georgia's old county unit system of state electoral districts violated the rights of inhabitants in the more populous Georgia counties.[6] Moreover, the system of bonus votes began in both parties because the South was then a one-party area. In 1916 the Republicans added bonus votes to reward areas outside the South where their party was successful. The Democrats later added bonus votes, partly in order to mollify the South for other reasons.

Finally, in November 1971 a group of young progressive Repub-

5. See *Congressional Record*, daily ed., Vol. 116 (March 26, 1970), pp. H2545–48.
6. *Gray* v. *Sanders*, 372 U.S. 368 (1963), and *Wesberry* v. *Sanders*, 376 U.S. 1 (1964).

licans sued their national party over its convention apportionment formula and called on the Republican National Committee to adopt a formula almost exactly like the controversial one that the Democratic National Committee had approved and defended in court. The GOP plaintiffs—members of the Ripon Society, an organization of Republican intellectuals—said that the Republican formula for 1972 discriminated against the more populous states and their voters, giving them fewer votes at the convention than their percentage of the national vote total warranted. The Ripon Society asked that a new apportionment formula be used for 1972 that would allocate 60 percent of the convention votes on the basis of each state's 1968 Republican presidential vote and 40 percent on the basis of every state's electoral vote.

What exactly are the apportionment formulas that have caused such concern since the days of William Howard Taft? What are their implications in terms of voting power? What alternative ways are there of allocating the votes?

The Republican Party

The Republican apportionment system is explicitly set forth in the rules that will govern the 1972 GOP convention, which were adopted, in conformity with the party's usual practice, at the previous national convention. Convention votes will be awarded to each state on the following bases:

1. Four delegates at large.

2. Two additional delegates at large for each congressman at large.

3. Six additional delegates at large to each state that in the last election cast a majority of its electoral votes for the Republican presidential ticket *or* elected a Republican United States senator *or* a Republican governor *or* a delegation to the House of Representatives that was more than half Republican in 1968 or 1970, or in a special election.

4. One district delegate to each congressional district that cast

at least 4,000 votes for the GOP presidential ticket in the previous election *or* for the Republican nominee for Congress in the preceding congressional election.

5. An additional district delegate to those congressional districts that cast at least 12,500 votes for the Republican nominee for either the presidency or the House in the last election. Since congressional districts were reapportioned on the basis of the 1970 census, each state that lost or gained a congressional district accordingly will lose or gain district votes at the 1972 GOP convention.

6. Finally, the District of Columbia will have nine delegates at large; it would have received an additional three delegates at large if in the 1968 election it had cast a majority of its electoral votes for the Republican presidential nominee. Puerto Rico will have five delegates at large; the Virgin Islands, three; and Guam, three. Table 2-1 shows a state-by-state breakdown of this formula.

The Republican apportionment formula thus has changed only incrementally since 1952—in the number of votes awarded for each factor in the system and in the addition for the 1972 convention of a predominantly Republican House delegation as another basis for awarding bonus votes. The principle of bonus votes to reward support for the party was established in the wake of the disastrous 1912 convention. This is the only major change that has ever been made in GOP convention apportionment. The Ripon Society suit is the only perceptible Republican counterpart to the Democratic reformers' effort to alter the party formula; fewer Republicans than Democrats are concerned about apportionment, and their concern came much later. Apparently most Republicans are satisfied with their system.

What are the political implications of the Republican apportionment formula? Three factors are represented in it: sovereignty, population, and party voting. State sovereignty is represented by the four at-large votes given each state, which in the 1972 convention will amount to 200 votes; plus the 10 votes for congressmen at large;[7] plus the 20 votes allocated to the territories and the District of Columbia. For the 1972 Republican convention, this factor amounts to 230 votes, or 17.1 percent of the convention total of 1,347 votes.

Unless the courts require the Republicans to reapportion their votes, population in the 1972 convention will be represented under the formula for district delegates. The original reason for awarding one delegate to each district that cast a fixed minimum of Republican votes (now 4,000) and an additional delegate to districts casting another, higher minimum (now 12,500) was to reward party voting. Put another way, the idea was to avoid the apportionment problem faced in the 1912 Republican convention. However, the number of GOP popular votes required for the allocation of convention votes has not been increased rapidly enough to keep pace with population growth and Republican strength: even in the three-way 1968 presidential race, there was *no* congressional district in the nation that did not cast at least 4,000 votes for Richard M. Nixon. Only two districts failed to cast 12,500 votes for the 1968 Republican presidential nominee and for the party's congressional nominee in 1970. Of these districts, one was in George C. Wallace's Alabama, and one in Mississippi. Essentially, then, the district formula must be regarded as in effect rewarding population size—the basis of House districting—rather than party voting. In the 1972 Republican convention, the 859 district votes will account for 63.8 percent of the total convention votes.

Party voting will be represented at the 1972 Republican convention by the at-large bonus votes granted to states that went Republican for President in 1968 or elected a Republican governor or United States senator or a predominantly Republican delegation to the House of Representatives in 1968 or 1970. Altogether the 258 bonus votes will represent 19.2 percent of the total convention

7. These ten votes must be assigned somewhat arbitrarily. It is argued here that assurance of a minimum of one vote in the House is primarily a recognition of the sovereignty of the state rather than of the population that it represents.

TABLE 2-1. *Apportionment of Votes at the 1972 Republican National Convention*

State or territory (total votes)	Four votes at large for each state	Two votes at large for each congressman at large	Six votes at large for states going Republican[a]	Basis for apportioning votes		District votes added or subtracted by reapportionment after census	Non-states
				One district vote for 4,000 Republican votes for President or for House[b]	One additional district vote for 12,500 Republican votes for President or for House[b]		
Alabama (18)	4	—	—	8	8	−2	—
Alaska (12)	4	2	6	—	—	—	—
Arizona (18)	4	—	6	3	3	+2	—
Arkansas (18)	4	—	6	4	4	—	—
California (96)	4	—	6	38	38	+10	—
Colorado (20)	4	—	6	4	4	+2	—
Connecticut (22)	4	—	6	6	6	—	—
Delaware (12)	4	2	6	—	—	—	—
Florida (40)	4	—	—	12	12	+6	—
Georgia (24)	4	—	—	10	10	—	—
Hawaii (14)	4	—	6	2	2	—	—
Idaho (14)	4	—	6	2	2	—	—
Illinois (58)	4	—	6	24	24	—	—
Indiana (32)	4	—	6	11	11	—	—
Iowa (22)	4	—	6	7	7	−2	—
Kansas (20)	4	—	6	5	5	—	—
Kentucky (24)	4	—	6	7	7	—	—
Louisiana (20)	4	—	—	8	8	—	—
Maine (8)	4	—	—	2	2	—	—
Maryland (26)	4	—	6	8	8	—	—
Massachusetts (34)	4	—	6	12	12	—	—
Michigan (48)	4	—	6	19	19	—	—
Minnesota (26)	4	—	6	8	8	—	—
Mississippi (13)	4	—	—	5	4	—	—
Missouri (30)	4	—	6	10	10	—	—

State (electoral votes)							
Montana (14)	4	—	6	2	2	—	—
Nebraska (16)	4	—	6	3	3	—	—
Nevada (12)	4	2	6	—	—	—	—
New Hampshire (14)	4	—	6	2	2	—	—
New Jersey (40)	4	—	6	15	15	—	—
New Mexico (14)	4	—	6	2	2	—	—
New York (88)	4	—	6	41	41	−4	—
North Carolina (32)	4	—	6	11	11	—	—
North Dakota (12)	4	—	6	2	2	−2	—
Ohio (56)	4	—	6	24	24	−2	—
Oklahoma (22)	4	—	6	6	6	—	—
Oregon (18)	4	—	6	4	4	—	—
Pennsylvania (60)	4	—	6	27	27	−4	—
Rhode Island (8)	4	—	—	2	2	—	—
South Carolina (22)	4	—	6	6	6	—	—
South Dakota (14)	4	—	6	2	2	—	—
Tennessee (26)	4	—	6	9	9	−2	—
Texas (52)	4	—	—	23	23	+2	—
Utah (14)	4	—	6	2	2	—	—
Vermont (12)	4	2	6	—	—	—	—
Virginia (30)	4	—	6	10	10	—	—
Washington (24)	4	—	6	7	7	—	—
West Virginia (18)	4	—	6	5	5	−2	—
Wisconsin (28)	4	—	6	10	10	−2	—
Wyoming (12)	4	2	6	—	—	—	—
District of Columbia (9)	—	—	—	—	—	—	9[c]
Puerto Rico (5)	—	—	—	—	—	—	5
Virgin Islands (3)	—	—	—	—	—	—	3
Guam (3)	—	—	—	—	—	—	3
Total (1,347)	200	10	258	430	429	0	20

a. That is, six votes for each state that cast a majority of its electoral vote in 1968 for the Republican presidential nominee; *or* that elected a Republican senator, or governor, or a Republican majority of the state's delegation in the House in 1968 or subsequently.

b. In 1968 for President; in 1970 for representative.

c. The District of Columbia has nine delegates at large. It would have had three additional delegates at large if it had cast its electoral vote, or a majority thereof, for the Republican nominee in the last preceding presidential election.

votes. It should be emphasized that these bonus votes rewarding a state party for its success in carrying elections are based on a quite different theory of apportionment than are votes allocated according to the number of actual voters in a state who cast ballots for the party's candidates. The former system is based on victory; the latter, on the number of party voters. The Republican party has never made use of the latter apportionment method.

Thus the 1972 Republican formula very heavily represents population—potential voters—without much regard for the states in which they reside or their prior voting records. This is a recent development stemming from increased population and the growth of southern Republicanism. At the 1952 convention, for example, while every northern congressional district qualified for two district delegates, only 48 out of 105 southern districts had produced enough votes for Thomas E. Dewey in 1948 to qualify. Nor did support for Republican House candidates in 1950 provide any additional district votes for the South at the convention; indeed, there *were* only 29 GOP candidates for those 105 southern House seats in 1950. Under these circumstances, the district delegates that were allotted to southern states—though not those allotted to the North—*did* represent outstanding support for the party. The Eisenhower years wrought fundamental change in southern voting patterns. By 1960 Richard Nixon was able to gain enough popular votes to qualify every congressional district in the country, except three in Mississippi, for both district delegates at the 1964 Republican convention. Even the three Mississippi districts cast enough votes for Nixon to qualify for the initial district delegate. Realizing that change had occurred, the 1968 convention voted to increase the minimum number of votes necessary for district delegates; but the formula still lagged behind actual party voting patterns and resulted in the emphasis on population in the apportionment formula.

Another way of looking at changing political patterns within Republican conventions as a result of the apportionment formula is to consider the voting strength over time of various groups of states in the convention. Table 2-2 shows that there has been little variation in the twenty years 1952–72. The slight persistent shifts that do exist—notably the increasing strength of the South and the decreasing strength of New England—reflect fundamental population shifts throughout the nation and growing Republicanism in the South (offset somewhat in 1972 by George Wallace's showing in 1968).

TABLE 2-2. *Voting Strength of Selected Groups of States, as a Percentage of Total, at Republican National Conventions, 1952–72*

Group	1952	1956	1960	1964	1968	1972
Ten most populous states[a]	44.6	42.0	41.6	43.6	42.8	42.5
Ten least populous states[a]	10.5	10.0	9.2	9.0	8.9	9.5
South[b]	15.9	20.9	21.0	21.3	23.3	21.9
New England[c]	9.1	8.8	8.7	8.0	7.4	7.3
Rocky Mountain area[d]	8.8	8.5	8.4	8.3	8.1	8.8

a. At the time of the immediately preceding census.
b. Alabama, Arkansas, Florida, Georgia, Louisiana, Mississippi, North Carolina, South Carolina, Tennessee, Texas, and Virginia.
c. Connecticut, Maine, Massachusetts, New Hampshire, Rhode Island, and Vermont.
d. Arizona, Colorado, Idaho, Montana, Nevada, New Mexico, Utah, and Wyoming.

The Democratic Party

In recent years, apportionment has been a much more troublesome undertaking for the Democrats than for the Republicans. Because the Democrats never had a controversy like the one the Republicans had in 1912, the party of Andrew Jackson did not add bonus votes for party support to the customary electoral college apportionment basis until the 1944 Democratic convention. And they did so then only to fulfill promises that had been made to the South when the two-thirds rule for nomination was reduced to a simple majority in 1936.

The reasons for apportionment controversies in later years are not hard to find. In the first place, the Democratic party is composed of an unusually heterogeneous collection of groups and interests that compete against one another for leadership of the party.

The party's various factions—white southerners, blacks, Jews, Catholics, labor unions, urban organizations, and intellectuals— are *not* natural allies and in some cases are even natural enemies. Particularly with the increasing bitterness and salience of the race issue and more recently the Vietnam war, the various factions have become more suspicious of who is gaining the upper hand in running the party. The Democrats' inability since 1952 to translate consistently a large lead in mass popularity into successful presidential candidacies has added to the party's internal frustration and strife.

The way in which the apportionment formula is decided may also contribute to the differences between the parties. The Republicans approve their formula, as a part of the entire set of convention rules, four years in advance. Thus the Republican apportionment formula for 1972 was approved by the 1968 convention. Not so with the Democrats. The apportionment rules are decided not by the convention assembled but by the Democratic National Committee, and only a year or so before the convention that they govern. This means that the political implications of the various apportionment formulas being considered are much clearer in the Democratic decision-making process. As a result, representatives of the various states are far better able to think in terms of their state's particular political advantages and disadvantages under the plans being considered. They know, for example, whether the Democratic ticket carried their state in the last presidential election. If it did, and other factors are approximately equal, they are likely to favor an apportionment system that awards a maximum number of votes to states carried by the Democratic ticket. Otherwise, they probably will be less enthusiastic about the plan. In either case, conflict is more likely in a 110-member national committee with relatively few important duties than in a huge convention whose principal job is nominating candidates for President and Vice President.

A brief look at the way the Democrats' apportionment formulas have changed over the past twenty years shows constant factional jockeying for power within the party. The most populous and most Democratic states have been increasingly predominant, but the others have sought to protect their interests. In 1952, two groups of states stood to lose strength in the convention if it used the 1948 apportionment rule—two votes to every state for each of its United States senators and representatives, plus four bonus votes if the state had been carried by the Truman-Barkley ticket in 1948, and additional votes for the District of Columbia and the territories of Alaska, Hawaii, the Canal Zone, and the Virgin Islands. Under this system, the once solidly Democratic states of Alabama, Louisiana, Mississippi, and South Carolina, which had supported the States' Rights party ticket in the 1948 presidential election, would lose proportionate convention strength along with their bonus votes. Meanwhile, nine states were in the process of losing seats in the House—and putative convention votes—because of the decline in relative population revealed in the 1950 census. In response to pleas from the spokesmen for these states and from others who wanted to bring the South back into the party fold, the Democratic National Committee, while readopting the 1948 allocation formula for 1952, specifically provided that each state was entitled to no less than the same number of *delegates* it had in 1948.

Perennially dissatisfied with the apportionment formula, the Democratic National Committee proceeded to change it substantially for nearly every convention in the years that followed. For 1956, the national committee gave each state all the votes it had in 1952, plus four bonus votes to those states that had cast their electoral votes for Stevenson or had elected a Democratic governor or United States senator in 1952 or 1954. The 1960 formula allocated each state two and one-half votes for every United States senator or representative (the total to be rounded upward if necessary to the next higher whole number), plus a half vote for each member of the Democratic National Committee and additional votes if needed to match its 1956 vote total. For 1964 another new formula awarded each state three votes for every presidential elector (that is, for each United States senator and representative), plus one vote for every 100,000 popular votes "or major portion thereof" cast for the Kennedy-Johnson ticket in 1960, plus ten bonus votes for the states that were carried by that ticket,[8] plus a personal and nontransferable vote for each member of the Democratic National Committee, plus additional votes and/or delegates if necessary to equal the state's 1960 convention total. The formula for the 1968 convention was the same as for 1964 except that the states were not assured the same number of votes that they had had at the prior convention.

In the new debate about conventions following the 1968 disaster, apportionment was the first major issue to be voted on by the Democratic National Committee. After two years of study, the party's O'Hara Commission on Rules voted to adopt a formula based one-half on state population and one-half on the average Democratic vote for President in the state in the three previous elections. The District of Columbia also would have been given votes on this basis; no votes were recommended for other areas that were not states. The executive committee of the Democratic National Committee, however, overruled the O'Hara Commission decision and approved a different formula. Each state was to receive three times its number of electoral college votes plus additional votes based on the average vote for the party's presidential ticket in the past three elections.[9] A handful of votes were also allocated to the territories. The electoral college factor was to count for 54 percent of the total convention votes and the presidential vote factor, 46 percent. This formula and seven other apportionment plans—one based on the electoral college alone, one strictly on population, one wholly on the Democratic vote for President, and various compromise formulas—were presented to the full Democratic National Committee, which endorsed the ex-

8. Five votes were specifically allocated to Alabama, which had split its eleven electoral votes in 1960, five going to Kennedy and six votes—of "unpledged" electors—going ultimately to Senator Harry F. Byrd of Virginia.
9. Only two elections could be averaged for the District of Columbia, whose residents could not vote for President in 1960; and only two were used for Alabama, where the Johnson ticket was not on the ballot in 1964.

ecutive committee's plan. The basic intraparty split lay between spokesmen for the smaller states and their traditionalist allies (who backed maximum perquisites for the state parties and their leaders) and the reformist faction, which supported a one-partisan-one-vote formula that would reward states loyal to the national ticket—mostly northern states with what the reformers considered to be liberal constituencies.

What have been the political implications of the apportionment rules of the Democratic party? Table 2-3 shows the breakdown of apportionment for the 1972 convention by states. Like its Republican counterpart, the Democratic formula that year awarded votes on the bases of state or territorial sovereignty, party voting, and population. Votes allocated on the basis of state sovereignty included (1) 459 of the 1,614 votes awarded under the rule that pro_vides for 3 votes for each presidential elector, since the District of Columbia has three electors and each of the fifty states has a minimum of three electors; plus (2) the 16 votes allocated to the territories of the Canal Zone, Guam, Puerto Rico, and the Virgin Islands. A total of 475 votes, 15.7 percent of the total of 3,016 convention votes, were thus allocated on a sovereignty basis.

A sharp upturn in the importance of the most populous states and an equivalent decline in that of less populous states also are reflected clearly in the 1972 Democratic formula. As Table 2-4 shows, these two groups of states accounted for fairly constant segments of the convention votes from 1952 through 1968, though the small states gained in the latter year because of the Johnson landslide in 1964. For 1972 the populous states gained sharply—by nearly 10 percentage points—and the sparsely populated states dropped by about 50 percent. This major change also affected the relative positions of the three regional groupings shown, although the lack of support for the 1968 presidential ticket in the South and the Rocky Mountain states is further reason for their smaller role in 1972.

For the 1972 convention, the votes allocated on the basis of population alone are 1,155 votes awarded under the rule of 3 votes

TABLE 2-3. *Apportionment of Votes at the 1972 Democratic National Convention*

State or territory	Votes based on number of electors	Votes based on support of Democratic presidential candidates[a]	Total votes
Alabama	27	10	37
Alaska	9	1	10
Arizona	18	7	25
Arkansas	18	9	27
California	135	136	271
Colorado	21	15	36
Connecticut	24	27	51
Delaware	9	4	13
Florida	51	30	81
Georgia	36	17	53
Hawaii	12	5	17
Idaho	12	5	17
Illinois	78	92	170
Indiana	39	37	76
Iowa	24	22	46
Kansas	21	14	35
Kentucky	27	20	47
Louisiana	30	14	44
Maine	12	8	20
Maryland	30	23	53
Massachusetts	42	60	102
Michigan	63	69	132
Minnesota	30	34	64
Mississippi	21	4	25
Missouri	36	37	73
Montana	12	5	17
Nebraska	15	9	24
Nevada	9	2	11
New Hampshire	12	6	18
New Jersey	51	58	109
New Mexico	12	6	18
New York	123	155	278
North Carolina	39	25	64
North Dakota	9	5	14
Ohio	75	78	153

TABLE 2-3. *Continued*

State or territory	Basis for apportioning votes		Total votes
	Votes based on number of electors	Votes based on support of Democratic presidential candidates[a]	
Oklahoma	24	15	39
Oregon	18	16	34
Pennsylvania	81	101	182
Rhode Island	12	10	22
South Carolina	24	8	32
South Dakota	12	5	17
Tennessee	30	19	49
Texas	78	52	130
Utah	12	7	19
Vermont	9	3	12
Virginia	36	17	53
Washington	27	25	52
West Virginia	18	17	35
Wisconsin	33	34	67
Wyoming	9	2	11
District of Columbia	9	6	15
Puerto Rico	—	—	7
Canal Zone	—	—	3
Virgin Islands	—	—	3
Guam	—	—	3
Total	1,614	1,386	3,016

a. An average of each state's popular vote for Democratic presidential candidates in 1960, 1964, and 1968.

for each presidential elector from a state. (The 1,155 figure is the number left when the 459 allocated for at-large electors are subtracted from the total based on the number of electors—1,614.) These 1,155 votes based on population represent 38.3 percent of the total convention votes.

State party voting patterns for President account for 1,386 of the 1972 Democratic convention votes. Total votes based on party support in previous presidential elections were 46.0 percent of all convention votes.

The 1972 formula reflects the increasing importance and chang-

TABLE 2-4. *Voting Strength of Selected Groups of States, as a Percentage of Total, at Democratic National Conventions, 1952–72*

Group[a]	1952	1956	1960	1964	1968	1972
Ten most populous states	43.7	41.8	41.6	45.7	43.6	53.3
Ten least populous states	7.5	8.2	7.9	7.3	9.1	4.6
South	23.6	24.3	23.1	22.5	20.1	19.7
New England	7.2	7.6	7.5	7.9	8.3	7.5
Rocky Mountain area	7.8	8.7	8.4	6.6	7.7	4.9

a. See notes to Table 2-2.

ing definition of party voting in recent Democratic apportionment schemes. The Democrats did not allocate any votes as a reward for party support until the 1944 convention. Only bonus votes rewarding the state parties, and not votes based on the number of voters supporting the party nominee, were used until 1964. Even after a presidential victory in 1948, bonus votes accounted for a mere 9.4 percent of the 1952 Democratic convention votes. In 1956, after the Eisenhower victory of 1952, votes for governor and senator as well as for President were included in the bonus for supporting the Democrats; at the 1956 convention, bonus votes amounted to 18.7 percent of the total. In 1960, no votes were apportioned specifically on the basis of party voting. In 1964, bonus votes for the Kennedy ticket in 1960 accounted for 9.7 percent of the total national convention votes and party voters for an additional 12.7 percent. By 1968, bonus votes accounted for 17.2 percent and party voters 16.5 percent of the votes at the Democratic convention. In 1972, bonus votes were eliminated, and 46.0 percent of the convention votes were based directly on the number of voters who supported the party's presidential ticket in the three previous elections. Party voting—and particularly the number of party voters—thus appears to be emerging as the major factor in Democratic apportionment formulas. Given its absence from the 1960 formula, however, the trend is as yet unstable.

Politically, then, apportionment formulas of the two parties are studies in contrast. Their schemes for 1972 differ significantly. Party voting is a much more important factor for the Democrats, and population accounts for a considerably larger segment of the

Republican convention votes, with territorial sovereignty of equal weight in the two parties, for all practical purposes. Again the Republican formula, essentially unchanged, has reflected since 1952 little dramatic shift in the voting strength of various groups of states within the convention; in the Democratic conventions during the same period there have been major shifts.

Why the difference? The varying traditions, internal situations, and strategic positions of the two parties account for the divergent patterns. The Republicans reformed their apportionment system to accommodate their situation in the South after 1912. Since then, there has been little perceptible agitation within the party for a new system. Although the letter of the present rule for district delegates has diverged from its original intent as minimum Republican strength has become national, many Republicans may believe, because of the rule's derivation and language, that it gives greater weight to party voting than it actually does. The Democrats, in contrast, have been perennially and notoriously divided, with northern liberals, southern conservatives, spokesmen for small states, and other factions all openly seeking advantage within the party by way of the apportionment system.

The differing strategic situations of a minority and a majority party may further account for the variation between the parties. With relatively fewer supporters in the electorate, the Republicans need to attract votes. One way is to strengthen the nascent Republican parties in southern states; providing them the reward of district delegates at the conventions presumably helps do this. But to win a presidential election the Republicans also need to carry the competitive populous states in addition to the smaller ones in which they are normally predominant. Their apportionment formula serves this purpose by allocating nearly half the votes to the most populous states. This gives the GOP leaders in these states a major stake in presidential politics, although not as great a proportion of the total as they have in the electoral college, in the national population, and in votes for the presidential nominee at least in winning years.

On the other hand, the Democrats as the majority party need

only to receive active support from their own adherents in order to win. But they do need to hold those adherents; and the imminent collapse of the New Deal coalition has been predicted for years. Hence the multifarious Democratic factions have scrambled to keep their supporters. The increasing importance of the party support factor in their apportionment formulas suggests that the Democrats are emphasizing a holding action rather than creating a new coalition. If they should become the minority party, convention apportionment based primarily on population rather than on party support might appear more appealing to them.

Alternative Plans for Allocating Votes

In addition to the complex formulas actually used by the parties, there are four principal ways of apportioning convention votes. One is a foreign system that has never been used in the United States; others are systems based entirely on population by states and on party voting by states; finally, there are various mixed systems.

REPRESENTATION OF PARTY GROUPS AND OFFICIALS

It is possible to apportion convention votes in a way completely different from recent Republican and Democratic practice. In Canada, constituent party groups are directly represented. As Carl Baar has noted,[10] the Canadian Liberal and Conservative parties apportion convention votes directly to members of, or defeated candidates for, parliament and the provincial legislatures; members of the federal privy council and the federal senate; members of the national party executive and of the standing committee of the national party federation; provincial party leaders, senior executives, and women's and youth organization leaders, and lead-

10. In "Party Organization, Convention Organization and Leadership Selection in Canada and the United States," paper delivered at the sixty-sixth annual meeting of the American Political Science Association in Los Angeles, California, Sept. 11, 1970.

ers of university party organizations. Baar rightly points out that even when debating major reforms, the two parties in the United States have not seriously considered apportioning convention votes directly to party officials and groups as such. In the United States, the national parties are essentially coalitions of state parties, and conventions are organized accordingly. Moreover, U.S. conventions are viewed as convocations of representatives chosen specifically as delegates and not because of their prominence in other political or governmental offices.

While the Canadian pattern is most unlikely to be adopted by either party in the United States, it is worthy of contemplation. State delegations need not necessarily be the basic organizational unit of national nominating conventions; party-related organizations may serve the purpose. Delegates need not be elected; certain categories of public officials and party leaders may be granted ex officio voting rights at the convention, as members of the Democratic National Committee have been in several years.

The lack of serious attention to the Canadian experience during the contemporary debate about conventions in the United States has occurred because the current reform movement stresses representation of the rank and file, especially *party voters*. It is suspicious of established party organizations and their presumed oligarchical tendencies. Where the Canadian pattern would introduce the new perspectives of specialized national constituencies into the nominating conventions through the apportionment system, reformers in the United States have sought instead to provide adequate representation for categories excluded from, or minimized in, the traditional delegate selection process—blacks, other minority groups, youth, women, and so on. To these reformers, allocating votes to representatives of party organizations is an elitist system. It also produces delegates who are responsible primarily to their specialized national constituencies, rather than to the party rank and file. In addition there is no definite assurance that at Canadian-style conventions the spokesmen for youth, for example, would be present in numbers commensurate with the strength of the young in the party-at-the-polls or in the population at large. Thus, while the Canadian system may have merits, it also creates dilemmas; and it does not emphasize the values of the current reform movement in the United States.

REPRESENTATION OF POPULATION BY STATES

The first rules actually used for apportioning national party conventions in the United States provided that each state should have as many votes as it had presidential electors (its number of United States senators and representatives). The representation of population by states is still a major factor in convention apportionment. Although there is scant sentiment today for a return to representation according to the electoral college formula alone, there is considerable political support for maintaining electoral college representation as an element in the overall apportionment scheme.

The electoral college representation principle is backed by those who want to protect the interests of small states. Historically, the idea of allotting to each state two United States senators and at least one representative—more of the latter when the state's population justified it—was intended by the framers of the Constitution to balance two kinds of interests. Representation in the Senate recognized the principle of equal sovereignty for all states; that in the House, the principle of representation according to a state's number of inhabitants. This compromise was simply carried over into the electoral college system for electing the President. However, there is a very crucial difference in the way the electoral college has operated recently. The large states actually have been preeminent in the system because a state casts all its votes in a bloc for the party ticket that carries it. This means that in 1968, for example, New York cast a total of forty-five electoral votes for Hubert H. Humphrey and Edmund S. Muskie, whereas Alaska cast a total of only three for Richard M. Nixon and Spiro T. Agnew. Thus the most populous states, those with large metropolitan areas, have dominated the electoral college since the general-ticket, or winner-take-all, system became standard procedure in the mid-nineteenth century. This is not so in Congress; while Congress is actually apportioned in the same way, each member votes as an individual and not specifically as part of a united state bloc.

In contemporary presidential nominating conventions, this system of apportionment would work more nearly as it does in Congress than as in the electoral college. This is because of the voting rules. The national Republican party has never enforced a state unit rule for voting at conventions; each member of each state delegation always has been free, at least theoretically, to vote as he or she chooses, subject only to obligations to his or her constituency and political pressures. Many state Democratic parties, however, long operated under the unit rule, by which all of a state's votes were cast for the candidate or viewpoint with the most support within the state delegation. Many state party leaders, particularly in the South, favored the unit rule because it gave their state a united front and the strongest possible influence in relation to other states. Gradually, however, state delegations began abandoning the unit rule as undemocratic. At the 1968 Democratic convention, the national party approved a resolution formally banning the unit rule at all party levels for the 1972 national convention.

Yet regardless of whether the delegates vote as individuals or as part of state units, the electoral college or congressional formula does not reflect state population very accurately. It systematically overrepresents the smaller states by including in the basis of apportionment two at-large "senatorial" votes and a minimum of one additional "House" vote.

A more precise formula for allocating votes on the basis of state population would be one based on the principle of one-inhabitant-one-vote. Votes would be apportioned according to the number of people officially counted in each state in the last decennial census. This would right the balance in population terms as between the larger states and the smaller states. It would ensure that all enumerated Americans were represented as equally as possible within the framework of a federal system of convention apportionment.

Yet the one-inhabitant-one-vote formula contains significant biases. For a variety of reasons, some of the national population—more than a statistical trace—is not counted in the census. Those not enumerated are believed to be predominantly from the lower strata of American society. Also, (because the federal census is taken only every ten years, its figures are often several years in arrears of population shifts. Areas of rapid population growth are thereby penalized; states that lose population are overrepresented at least until the next census.)In addition, one-inhabitant-one-vote is not the same as one-voter-one-vote. Not all inhabitants are citizens, not all are eligible to vote, not all are registered voters, and not all of those registered actually vote. The one-inhabitant-one-vote formula gives no weight to the relative strength of a party within a state.)

REPRESENTATION OF PARTY VOTING BY STATES

The vanguard of reformers in the current debate about conventions believe (that national party conventions should directly represent members of the party at the grassroots level, and hence they favor an apportionment system based on party voting by state.) The basis for their position is usually one-partisan-one-vote.) While there are various ways of working out the arithmetic, the principle remains the same. As has been noted, another system also based on party voting, but very different in terms of internal party politics, is that of (awarding a fixed number of bonus convention votes to states that have supported the party ticket.)

(The one-partisan-one-vote formula is readily understandable. A party simply would set the overall number of convention votes and then allocate them among the states in proportion to their share of the party's popular strength nationwide.)The benchmark could be the previous presidential election, or the average vote in several presidential elections or in elections for other offices. Alternatively, there could be no fixed number of convention votes, but instead/each state could be awarded one convention vote for a fixed number of party voters—one vote, for example, for each 50,000 voters in a particular election or averaged over a group of elections.)

This one-partisan-one-vote formula, of course, has political implications very different from those of the apportionment system based on population by state. The plan using a party-voters standard would tend to reward the larger states, the states with higher turnout, and naturally the states most loyal to the party, in the years and for the offices included in the formula. An apportionment plan based only on party voters also would fluctuate more from convention to convention than would a plan based on population, since voting trends vary more sharply and are officially measured more frequently than population trends.

(Another and quite different system of rewarding party voting is to allocate a certain number of bonus votes to each state carried by the party. This method has been used (though obviously never as the only method) by both the Democrats and the Republicans in recent years. Because it awards a fixed number of votes to each state in which the party wins, this system overrepresents smaller states on the basis of both their number of party voters and their population.)

The theoretical issue involved in assessing the formula based on party voting by states—either the one-partisan-one-vote plan or the plan rewarding loyal states—concerns the nature of a political party. Ironically, the Democratic reformers are arguing in this instance for privatization of the party. Basing representation on party voting alone implies that only those who vote for the ticket constitute the party. If so, are other citizens not to be represented at all? What of those who do not vote? What of those who shift between the parties? And what of the loyal partisans who do not like the candidate? (Basing apportionment on partisanship alone would permit control of the national convention over time to be gained by a faction that successively nominated the candidates most satisfactory to its own constituency. This would mean that the faction would earn more and more convention votes and that the party's base would be correspondingly narrower. The ultimate and perhaps rapid result of such a pattern would be defeat and perhaps destruction of the party. Similarly, the minority party might be consigned to that status permanently.

Advocates of apportionment plans based on party voting contend that party supporters are the true constituency of party conventions: "In a party assembly total population is not directly relevant."[11] Or as Democratic National Committeeman John F. English of New York, a proponent of a one-partisan-one-vote plan, said: "We don't mind having trees represented, but now we have proposals that are going to reward Republicans as well as trees."[12] Moreover, the vote is the easiest and most reliable way to measure the number of loyalists in a state. Purists who favor the party-voting standard probably would argue further that the party, while by definition composed of active supporters, is nonetheless open to all who care to cast a ballot for it.

The more flexible proponents of representation based on party voting by states would be willing to concede the quasi-public character and fundamentally expansionist needs of the political party by tempering the representation of partisans with additional representation based on state population. Some would also permit a certain number of votes to be based on territorial sovereignty in order not to overwhelm the smallest states.

MIXED APPORTIONMENT SYSTEMS

The apportionment systems actually used by the parties in recent years have combined representation of population, party voters, and territorial sovereignty. The political implications of these systems and their alternatives remain to be considered.

Tables 2-5 and 2-6 compare the effects of alternative plans. They show what would be the voting strength of the states and

11. David, Goldman, and Bain, *The Politics of National Party Conventions*, p. 178.
12. Quoted in the *New York Times*, Feb. 20, 1971, p. 12.

territories at the 1972 Republican and Democratic conventions under four different systems for allocating the votes. The systems are (1) the actual 1972 Republican and Democratic formulas, (2) a formula based on 1970 population, (3) the 1972 electoral college formula, and (4) a formula based on the percentage of the party's total presidential vote in 1968 that was contributed by each state.

Clearly, different apportionment formulas do imply different voting strengths for individual states. Table 2-5 indicates sharp differences for the Republicans. Depending on the formula used, Delaware's voting strength would vary from 0.2 percent to 0.9 percent—small in absolute terms, but relatively a matter of a 350 percent increase. For New York, the formula used could mean the difference between 6.5 percent and 9.6 percent of the votes. According to Table 2-6 Alabama would have 1.7 percent of the total votes at the Democratic convention if the 1970 population or 1972 electoral college formulas were used; but it would have only 0.6 percent of the total votes if support for the Humphrey-Muskie ticket were the sole criterion for apportionment. Again, California would have 10.4 percent of the total convention votes if support for the 1968 Democratic nominees were the basis for apportionment but only 8.4 percent if the 1972 electoral college formula were used by the Democrats.

Tables 2-7 and 2-8 spell out the differences between the formulas in more categoric terms, showing the shares of the ten most populous states, the ten least populous states, and three regions: the South, New England, and the Rocky Mountain states. The comparisons indicate differences between the parties as well as among the plans.

In the Republican party (see Table 2-7) the most populous states would be strongest (with 57.1 percent of the votes) under the plan based solely on support for the Nixon-Agnew ticket in 1968, and weakest—although still controlling 42.5 percent of the convention votes—under the formula that the Republicans will use for 1972. The least populous states would be relatively strongest

TABLE 2-5. *Voting Strength of the States at the 1972 Republican National Convention under Various Apportionment Formulas*
Percent

	Basis for apportioning votes			
State or territory	Actual 1972 Republican formula	1970 Population	1972 Electoral College	Percentage of 1968 Nixon vote total
Alabama	1.3	1.7	1.7	0.4
Alaska	0.9	0.1	0.6	0.1
Arizona	1.3	0.9	1.1	0.7
Arkansas	1.3	0.9	1.1	0.6
California	7.1	9.8	8.4	11.0
Colorado	1.5	1.1	1.3	1.3
Connecticut	1.6	1.5	1.5	1.8
Delaware	0.9	0.2	0.6	0.3
Florida	3.0	3.4	3.2	2.6
Georgia	1.8	2.3	2.2	1.1
Hawaii	1.0	0.4	0.7	0.3
Idaho	1.0	0.3	0.7	0.5
Illinois	4.3	5.5	4.8	6.9
Indiana	2.4	2.6	2.4	3.4
Iowa	1.6	1.4	1.5	2.0
Kansas	1.5	1.1	1.3	1.5
Kentucky	1.8	1.6	1.7	1.4
Louisiana	1.5	1.8	1.9	0.8
Maine	0.6	0.5	0.7	0.5
Maryland	1.9	1.9	1.9	1.7
Massachusetts	2.5	2.8	2.6	2.4
Michigan	3.6	4.4	3.9	4.3
Minnesota	1.9	1.9	1.9	2.0
Mississippi	1.0	1.1	1.3	0.3
Missouri	2.2	2.3	2.2	2.5
Montana	1.0	0.3	0.7	0.4
Nebraska	1.2	0.7	0.9	1.0
Nevada	0.9	0.2	0.6	0.2
New Hampshire	1.0	0.3	0.7	0.5
New Jersey	3.0	3.5	3.2	4.2
New Mexico	1.0	0.5	0.7	0.5
New York	6.5	8.9	7.6	9.6
North Carolina	2.4	2.5	2.4	2.0
North Dakota	0.9	0.3	0.6	0.4
Ohio	4.2	5.2	4.6	5.8

TABLE 2-5. *Continued*

State or territory	Basis for apportioning votes			
	Actual 1972 Republican formula	1970 Population	1972 Electoral College	Percentage of 1968 Nixon vote total
Oklahoma	1.6	1.3	1.5	1.5
Oregon	1.3	1.0	1.1	1.3
Pennsylvania	4.5	5.8	5.0	6.4
Rhode Island	0.6	0.5	0.7	0.4
South Carolina	1.6	1.3	1.5	0.8
South Dakota	1.0	0.3	0.7	0.4
Tennessee	1.9	1.9	1.9	1.5
Texas	3.9	5.5	4.8	3.9
Utah	1.0	0.5	0.7	0.8
Vermont	0.9	0.2	0.6	0.3
Virginia	2.2	2.3	2.2	1.9
Washington	1.8	1.7	1.7	1.7
West Virginia	1.3	0.9	1.1	1.0
Wisconsin	2.1	2.2	2.0	2.6
Wyoming	0.9	0.1	0.6	0.2
District of Columbia	0.7	0.4	0.6	0.1
Puerto Rico	0.4	—	0.0	0.0
Virgin Islands	0.2	—	0.0	0.0
Guam	0.2	—	0.0	0.0
Rounded total	100.0	100.0	100.0	100.0

(9.5 percent) under the 1972 Republican formula, and relatively weakest (3.3 percent) under a formula based strictly on population. Among the regions, the South would be at its peak of voting strength (24.2 percent of the total convention votes) under the electoral college formula, and at the greatest disadvantage (16.1 percent) under the Nixon-support criterion. New England would have a high of 7.3 percent of the votes under the actual Republican formula for 1972 and a low of 5.8 percent under the population formula and the Nixon-support plan. The Rocky Mountain states would have a maximum of 8.8 percent under the official Republican

TABLE 2-6. *Voting Strength of the States at the 1972 Democratic National Convention under Various Apportionment Formulas*
Percent

	Basis for apportioning votes			
State or territory	Actual 1972 Democratic formula	1970 Population	1972 Electoral College	Percentage of 1968 Humphrey vote total
Alabama	1.2	1.7	1.7	0.6
Alaska	0.3	0.1	0.6	0.1
Arizona	0.8	0.9	1.1	0.5
Arkansas	0.9	0.9	1.1	0.6
California	9.0	9.8	8.4	10.4
Colorado	1.2	1.1	1.3	1.1
Connecticut	1.7	1.5	1.5	2.0
Delaware	0.4	0.2	0.6	0.3
Florida	2.7	3.4	3.2	2.2
Georgia	1.8	2.3	2.2	1.1
Hawaii	0.6	0.4	0.7	0.5
Idaho	0.6	0.3	0.7	0.3
Illinois	5.6	5.5	4.8	6.5
Indiana	2.5	2.6	2.4	2.6
Iowa	1.5	1.4	1.5	1.5
Kansas	1.2	1.1	1.3	1.0
Kentucky	1.6	1.6	1.7	1.3
Louisiana	1.5	1.8	1.9	1.0
Maine	0.7	0.5	0.7	1.0
Maryland	1.8	1.9	1.9	1.7
Massachusetts	3.4	2.8	2.6	4.7
Michigan	4.4	4.4	3.9	5.1
Minnesota	2.1	1.9	1.9	2.7
Mississippi	0.8	1.1	1.3	0.5
Missouri	2.4	2.3	2.2	2.5
Montana	0.6	0.3	0.7	0.4
Nebraska	0.8	0.7	0.9	0.5
Nevada	0.4	0.2	0.6	0.2
New Hampshire	0.6	0.3	0.7	0.4
New Jersey	3.6	3.5	3.2	4.0
New Mexico	0.6	0.5	0.7	0.4
New York	9.2	8.9	7.6	10.8
North Carolina	2.1	2.5	2.4	1.5
North Dakota	0.5	0.3	0.6	0.3
Ohio	5.1	5.2	4.6	5.4

TABLE 2-6. *Continued*

	Basis for apportioning votes			
State or territory	*Actual 1972 Democratic formula*	*1970 Population*	*1972 Electoral College*	*Percentage of 1968 Humphrey vote total*
Oklahoma	1.3	1.3	1.5	1.0
Oregon	1.1	1.0	1.1	1.1
Pennsylvania	6.0	5.8	5.0	7.2
Rhode Island	0.7	0.5	0.7	0.8
South Carolina	1.1	1.3	1.5	0.6
South Dakota	0.6	0.3	0.7	0.4
Tennessee	1.6	1.9	1.9	1.1
Texas	4.3	5.5	4.8	4.1
Utah	0.6	0.5	0.7	0.5
Vermont	0.4	0.2	0.6	0.2
Virginia	1.8	2.3	2.2	1.4
Washington	1.7	1.7	1.7	2.0
West Virginia	1.2	0.9	1.1	1.2
Wisconsin	2.2	2.2	2.0	2.4
Wyoming	0.4	0.1	0.6	0.1
District of Columbia	0.5	0.4	0.6	0.4
Puerto Rico	0.2	0.0	—	0.0
Canal Zone	0.1	0.0	—	0.0
Virgin Islands	0.1	0.0	—	0.0
Guam	0.1	0.0	—	0.0
Rounded total	100.0	100.0	100.0	100.0

formula and a minimum of 4.2 percent under the population formula.

In the Democratic party, as Table 2-8 indicates, the ten most populous states would control the largest share (60.6 percent) of the total convention votes under the formula based solely on support for the Democratic presidential ticket in 1968, and the smallest share (48.1 percent) under the electoral college formula. The ten least populous states would be relatively strongest (6.3 percent) under the electoral college formula and least strong (2.7 percent) under the Humphrey-support formula. The South would

TABLE 2-7. *Voting Strength of Selected Groups of States, as a Percentage of Total, at the 1972 Republican Convention, under Various Apportionment Formulas*

Group[a]	Republican formula, 1972	Population formula[b]	Electoral College formula, 1972	Nixon-support (1968) formula
Ten most populous states	42.5	54.9	48.1	57.1
Ten least populous states	9.5	3.3	6.3	3.5
South	21.9	19.1	24.2	16.1
New England	7.3	5.8	6.9	5.8
Rocky Mountain states	8.8	4.2	6.5	4.8

a. See notes to Table 2-2.

b. Based on memorandum of the Democratic National Committee's Commission on Rules, dated January 1971. The other calculations are the author's.

benefit most (24.2 percent) under the electoral college formula and least (14.6 percent) under the plan based on support for the Democratic presidential ticket in 1968. New England's strength would vary from 5.8 percent of the convention total under the population formula to 8.8 percent under the Humphrey-support plan. The Rocky Mountain states would have only 3.5 percent of the votes under the Humphrey-support formula but 6.5 percent under the electoral college formula.

These tables, of course, are suggestive rather than definitive. Politics is in a constant state of flux, and plans that would re-

TABLE 2-8. *Voting Strength of Selected Groups of States, as a Percentage of Total, at the 1972 Democratic Convention, under Various Apportionment Formulas*

Group[a]	Democratic formula, 1972	Population formula[b]	Electoral College formula, 1972	Humphrey-support (1968) formula
Ten most populous states	53.3	54.9	48.1	60.6
Ten least populous states	4.6	3.3	6.3	2.7
South	19.7	19.1	24.2	14.6
New England	7.5	5.8	6.9	8.8
Rocky Mountain states	4.9	4.2	6.5	3.5

a. See notes to Table 2-2.

b. Based on memorandum of the Democratic National Committee's Commission on Rules, dated January 1971. The other calculations are the author's.

ward one faction at one time might serve the interests of another at a different point. Factors like party support and population trends may change radically, depending on the time period used. Moreover, state delegations are unlikely to be united in a seriously contested convention, and so the categorical breakdowns in the tables do not represent predictable voting patterns. What the tables do show is that the choice of apportionment formula can make a decisive difference in terms of voting strength.

Determination of the most desirable apportionment formula or formulas hinges on a definition of party. If the people to be represented at the convention are those who voted for the party in the past, then obviously the appropriate formula would use that record as a benchmark. In the United States, with its federal system, party voting by state would be the form. But even here there are several different choices. Does the party-in-the-electorate consist of the party voters, or of the party workers who succeeded in mobilizing them to carry a state? If the former, then the standard should be one-partisan-one-vote; if the latter, then bonus votes are called for. And for which offices should the voting patterns be used? Should only the vote for President be included, under the theory that a *presidential* nominating convention is concerned? Or should other offices be included as well because it is a convention of the party's leaders throughout the nation? Should the national party leadership criterion alone be used, as it is in Canada? Or should the party-in-the-electorate idea be expanded to include potential voters by basing apportionment on population by state?[13]

The purpose of a convention apportionment formula is to provide representation for the party's presidential constituency. The party constituency of a presidential nominee is partly the actual constituency of predecessors and partly the potential constituency for that year. A formula that incorporates both factors was recommended by the Democrats' O'Hara Commission on Rules. It is

13. For statistical precision, the potential constituency would be a state's registered voters, rather than its population. Registration is still open at the time apportionment formulas are approved, however; as a result, population is a more convenient rule of thumb.

based 50 percent on each state's vote for President in the three preceding elections and 50 percent on population by state. Another formula, approved by the Democratic National Committee for 1972, is based approximately half on each state's popular vote for President in the last three elections and half on its electoral college votes. Using electoral votes as a measure of the party's presidential constituency is fair and reasonable so long as the electoral college system is maintained. But to be consistent, both the past number of electoral votes actually carried and the potential number that could be won in the future should be used in measuring the constituency. This solution is not politically feasible, and no one has recommended it publicly. It is not based on party voters. Hence, a formula based half on past presidential voting and half on population would be best.

Prospects for adoption of this formula are not particularly good. The Democrats appear to be moving in this direction. Given their past history of frequent change in apportionment methods, however, it is uncertain what they will do. The apportionment formula should be a permanent part of convention rules, amendable only by formal action of the assembly itself. The apportionment formula *is* that immutable in the Republican party; but it is not based directly on either party voters by state or population by state. While it is true that the vast majority of active Republicans seem satisfied with their time-honored formula, a broader spectrum of the citizenry has a stake in their party operations. Given the deliberate pace for changing Republican rules and the lack of interest in the Nixon White House—or indeed anywhere in the GOP except in the Ripon Society—for altering the apportionment formula, it is unrealistic to expect the Republicans to revise their formula in the near future. But if, as is argued here, the proper standard of representation at conventions is a combination of representation for state population and for party popular votes for President, there is no fair basis for requiring that standard only of the Democrats.

☆

Chapter Three

☆

SELECTING THE DELEGATES

*The Guidelines that we have adopted are designed to open the door
to all Democrats who seek a voice in their party's most important decision:
the choice of its presidential nominee.*
Commission on Party Structure and Delegate Selection,
Democratic National Committee

I would like the Republican party to be the party of the open door.
Richard M. Nixon

IF THE VIEWS of the party-in-the-electorate are to be fairly represented at the national convention, then procedures for selecting and seating delegates are of paramount importance. For it is the men and women actually taking part in the convention who cast votes in the name of the rank-and-file party adherents for presidential and vice presidential candidates, platforms, and party rules. The selection of convention delegates is the only link most Americans have with their representatives to the national party gathering; few citizens write, wire, or visit their often unknown spokesmen at the short-lived national convention, nor do delegates face the discipline of a re-election campaign.

Methods for choosing and seating delegates have provided a persistent issue during the past twenty years. As a result, both national parties—long concerned primarily with the extent to which each state party complied with its own provincial rules for choosing delegates—have adopted national standards for selecting delegates and have elaborated their procedures for contesting delegate credentials.

The character of the parties is defined partially by these processes. One indication of who holds authority in the party is *the
institution used for choosing delegates*—a party committee, a state or
local party caucus or convention, or a primary election. Another
indication of the party's internal makeup is provided by the *demographic characteristics of the delegates* who are selected—their race,
sex, age, and so on. Further, the *credentials challenge system* shows
the judgments by both the national party and the state and local
parties about who is entitled to participate in party affairs and
what constitutes fair procedure in party processes.

Institutions for Selecting Delegates

Aristotle would have conceded that delegate selection methods
defy rigorous classification. Formally, there are three ways: A
state's delegates may be appointed by party leaders, chosen at a
convention, or elected in a primary. As Table 3-1 shows, in 1968
most states used the convention method, and the fewest used the
appointment system. Also the largest number of delegates were
chosen by the convention procedure and the fewest, by appointment; but because many populous states held primaries, proportionately more delegates were selected by that system than the

TABLE 3-1. *Delegate Selection Methods Used in 1968*

	Appointment		Convention		Primary	
Party	Number	Percent	Number	Percent	Number	Percent
Democrats						
States using[a]	12	21.8	33	60.0	16	29.1
Total delegate votes[b]	327	12.9	1,227	46.4	1,068	40.7
Republicans						
States using[a]	4	7.5	37	69.8	15	28.3
Total delegate votes[b]	41	3.1	747	56.0	545	40.9

Sources: Democratic National Committee, Commission on Party Structure and Delegate
Selection, *Mandate for Reform* (1970), pp. 18, 22; Republican National Committee, *The
Process of Delegate Selection for the Republican National Convention, 1968* (1968).
    a. Details do not add to 100 percent because some states used more than one method.
    b. Because of fractional voting, data for the Democrats refer to votes only and not to
total delegates by state; Republican data refer equally to votes and to delegates.

state-by-state breakdown would imply. Of the two parties, the Republicans made substantially less use of the appointment system and more of the convention method.

The pattern for 1968 is typical of the recent era except that a larger number of states now use the primary system—twenty-two states and the District of Columbia in 1972—an increase of about 50 percent over the previous election. In 1972, at least half the delegates in each party will be elected in primaries. Most of the new primary states are of moderate size.

Unfortunately for those attempting to understand the political process, listing three delegate selection methods touches only the tip of the iceberg. Appointed delegates, for example, have been named by a variety of authorities. In several states in 1968, they were selected by the party's state central committee or its state executive committee. In other states, they were in effect chosen by the governor. In the Oklahoma Democratic party the delegates were picked by party committees in the various congressional districts. And in Wisconsin the Democratic delegation was selected by the party's state administrative committee and by Senator Eugene McCarthy, the winner of the presidential preference primary.

For obvious reasons, the appointment system has benefited whichever presidential candidates were supported by those already in power. Hence, it long aided candidates who emphasized an "inside" strategy of seeking the nomination by work through the party organizations (for example, Hubert Humphrey in 1968) rather than those stressing an "outside" strategy of public popularity and demonstrated strength in primaries. However, state and local leaders often have been persuaded that a candidate who ran well in the primaries would do similarly well in November. In any case, the day is probably gone when a candidate could hope to win by means of the inside strategy alone.

Within the meanings of the terms as used in Chapter 1, the party committee has been the least "fair" and "democratic" of the three institutions for selecting delegates. Often the state party officials charged with this authority have not themselves been chosen by party voters specifically for this purpose. When the party has had a governor in office, he has controlled the party committee and effectively named the delegates, who usually have been chosen for state or local reasons completely unrelated to the presidential race or national issues. Only persons acceptable to the governor—or, when the state party was out of power, acceptable to the faction in control of the party committee—have had a chance to be members of the national convention delegation. As a result, delegates have been estranged from the constituency that they nominally represent. For example, black delegates from Pennsylvania voted to seat the Lester Maddox delegation from Georgia rather than Julian Bond's insurgents at the 1968 Democratic convention.[1]

There is no realistic way to guarantee that appointed delegates will be responsive to the presidential preferences and other views on national issues of the party voters. A special state committee whose sole function was to select national convention delegates could be elected by the voters on the basis of their national views; but such a group would resemble more closely an electoral college than a party committee, and it is probably a utopian suggestion. In the interests of fairness and democracy, the appointment system ought to be eliminated. If that is not done, national standards should require at least that any party officials who appoint delegates should themselves be elected by party voters who are informed of the officials' role in selecting delegates.

Perhaps because it has been the most frequently used method of delegate selection, there has been an even more bewildering array of variations on the convention system. There have been state conventions, county conventions, congressional district conventions, and a combination of these. Delegates to state and local conventions have been selected in precinct primaries, in open local caucuses of party members, and by local party officials. And the votes at such conventions have been apportioned on the bases of population, party strength, and geography.

1. Ken Bode, "Democratic Party Reform," *New Republic*, Vol. 165 (July 10, 1971), p. 21.

Politically, conventions have provided advantages for presidential candidates who had enough money, and effective enough organizations, to send out delegate hunters who would appeal to the state and local party leaders who were influential at the conventions. These candidates have not always captured conventions, however, because the interests represented there were not necessarily susceptible to their appeals. The various leaders and ordinary delegates at state conventions might be preoccupied with more immediate concerns at the state and local levels. But if other factors were approximately equal, even a state or local boss would want to back a successful presidential candidate, and a good showing in state and local primaries or polls might be persuasive. The convention system has not favored inherently either the front-running presidential candidate or the less prominent hopefuls, although conventions often have supported the candidate who has appeared to be most popular with the state's voters.

Ideally, at a fair and democratic convention, delegates would be elected by party voters and be responsive to their views, particularly their presidential candidate preferences. Accordingly, they would select a similarly representative national convention delegation. Apportionment would be based on population and party voting rather than on geographic areas as such. Procedural rules would meet the standards for national conventions that are described in Chapter 4. Exclusionary and distorting devices like proxy voting and the winner-take-all unit rule would be forbidden.

The election of convention delegates in a party primary has taken an increasing number of forms as more states have opted for primaries since 1968. Delegates have been elected statewide, or in congressional districts, or in some combination of the two. Their selection has been made by the voters either in conjunction with a presidential preference primary or without one; and if there has been such a presidential poll, its result might or might not be binding on the delegates at the national convention. The presidential candidate favored by candidates for delegate might or might not be listed on the ballot; in California the individual members of the delegate slates pledged to each candidate are not named on the ballot. In a statewide primary, delegate seats might be allotted on a winner-take-all basis, as in California; or they might be allocated partly statewide and partly by congressional district; or they might be divided proportionately among the presidential candidates according to their relative showing, as many candidates who failed to win statewide have suggested. The presidential preference primary might include on the ballot all the serious candidates for the party nomination (as determined by some state official), or it might include only those candidates who chose to file in that state.

The political implications of the primary election method of selecting delegates have been as varied as the number of possible combinations in primary systems implies. While a primary generally has been considered more responsive to "the people" than to "the bosses," this is an oversimplification. Established leaders have influenced the kind of primaries that states would have. State leaders, and their local allies, might favor a winner-take-all statewide primary, where they could run a ticket of prominent partisans that was unbeatable by anyone else. Or state leaders could run an uncommitted slate or delegates pledged to a favorite son or daughter as a means of maintaining control. Again, some district party leaders, including incumbent and potential members of Congress, might prefer electing delegates at the district level, on the assumption that these leaders could exercise more influence there. Many reformers have believed that a contest at the district level is more democratic because it is closer to the voters than is a statewide contest; but it might simply be manipulated by different leaders.

In the presidential race, the primary has favored candidates with sufficient funds for an intensive campaign. Advertising, a staff, travel expenses, and such are costly. The front-runner in the presidential contest usually has needed to win primaries in order to stay ahead, and the other candidates have needed to win primaries to gather momentum. With a better chance to win but more at stake to lose, the front-runner probably has been at a relative disadvantage in primaries because they increase the opportunities to stumble. Less well-known candidates, with little to lose and much to gain, often have difficulty raising the funds needed for primary campaigns. Again, if there were many candidates and the primaries produced no clear popular choice, there might result a multiballot national convention and a compromise nominee.

Those who are skeptical of primaries (Harry Truman called them "eyewash") have often denigrated them as little more than personality contests; those who advocate primaries, like Senator Birch Bayh of Indiana,[2] have argued that on the contrary they mean that more attention is paid to the issues. Neither description is accurate for all primaries. Under some circumstances, party leaders and state convention delegates charged with selecting national convention delegates also might be at least as interested in the personalities of presidential candidates and the issues of the day as were the voters in primary elections.

The primary election method of selecting delegates is potentially the fairest and most democratic system; but it, too, has had serious imperfections in some instances. To be fair, a primary system should not exclude any partisan with the necessary age and residence qualifications from registering and voting; and these qualifications should be lenient enough to permit maximum participation by adult partisans who have lived in an area long enough to familiarize themselves with the candidates and the issues.[3] Naturally, intimidation of potential registrants and voters or counting the votes dishonestly should be considered unacceptable. In order to be democratic, a primary system should permit voters to select candidates for delegate whose presidential preference (including

---

2. Quoted in Andrew J. Glass and Jonathan Cottin, "Democratic Reform Drive Falters as Spotlight Shifts to Presidential Race," *National Journal* (June 19, 1971), p. 1294.

3. It is argued here that all voting should be open to any citizen at least 18 years old and a six-months resident of the state and locality. For statewide presidential primaries and presidential elections, residence requirements should be abolished altogether.

no preference) is clear; it should be listed on the ballot. In order
to maximize voter choice, each candidate should approve a single
slate of potential delegates. Write-in votes should be permitted in
order to allow voters a full range of choice. Favorite son and
daughter candidacies that preclude a race by national aspirants
should be discouraged.[4] Any system for dividing the popular votes
into delegate votes is fair and democratic so long as it faithfully
reflects the preference of the voters among presidential candidates,
as indicated in the primary.[5]

In sum, fairness and democracy in delegate selection is a matter
of specifics, indeed minutiae, rather than sweeping generalizations.
Fair and democratic procedures may be followed in various ways,
as described. The most important principle that should be observed under any system is that the presidential candidate preference of the party-in-the-electorate be reflected faithfully in the
delegation that it sends to the national convention. The appointment system should be discouraged because it is far removed from
the voters' choice.

Characteristics of the Delegates

Asked about his experiences as a national convention delegate,
an Indiana Republican reportedly answered, "Where did you go?
Out. What did you do? Nothing."[6] Nonetheless, the office of
delegate, which exists in limited supply, is sought eagerly by supporters of presidential candidates and by state and local politicians
desiring recognition. Competition for a place in the delegations
has accelerated with the dawning political consciousness of blacks,

4. Popular national candidates, however, can defeat or embarrass favorite sons.
Thus Robert F. Kennedy defeated Indiana Governor Roger E. Branigan in 1968, and
George C. Wallace in 1964 carried 42 percent of the vote against Maryland Senator
Daniel B. Brewster, President Johnson's stand-in.
5. Compare Manning J. Dauer, William A. F. Stephenson, Harry Macy, and
David Temple, "Toward a Model State Presidential Primary Law," *American
Political Science Review*, Vol. 50 (March 1956), pp. 138–53.
6. Quoted in David R. Derge, "Hoosier Republicans in Chicago," in Paul Tillett
(ed.), *Inside Politics: The 1960 Conventions* (Oceana Publications, 1962), p. 134.

Spanish-speaking citizens, other ethnic groups, the young, and women. These groups claim in their newly emerging political awareness that they have not had their rightful share of delegate seats.

Delegates to the 1968 conventions—and doubtless the earlier ones—were overwhelmingly affluent, white, male, and over thirty years of age. Table 3-2 shows the best available breakdown for 1968, collected by John W. Soule and James W. Clarke, relying on their own sample of 368 delegates and on a telephone survey by the Columbia Broadcasting System of nearly 90 percent of the delegates.[7] According to these data, the Republican convention was somewhat more white, less male, older, and richer than its

TABLE 3-2. *Characteristics of Delegates to the 1968 Democratic and Republican Conventions*
Percent

Item	Democrats	Republicans
Race		
White and other[a]	94	98
Black	6	2
Sex		
Male	87	83
Female	13	17
Age		
30 and under	18	9
31–40	30	27
41–50	31	32
Over 50	21	32
Annual income		
Under $10,000	13	12
$10,000–20,000	47	29
Over $20,000	40	60

Sources: Information on race and sex of delegates is from a survey by the Columbia Broadcasting System. Information on age and total annual income is from the Soule-Clarke survey. Both surveys are reported in John S. Soule and James W. Clarke, "The New Politics and the National Conventions" (unpublished manuscript), Chaps. 1 and 2.

Note: Details may not add to 100 percent due to rounding.

a. No data are available for Asians, American Indians, or other non-white groups.

7. John W. Soule and James W. Clarke, "The New Politics and the National Conventions" (unpublished manuscript), Chaps. 1 and 2.

Democratic counterpart. But the differences between the parties were minuscule compared to the vast gaps between blacks and whites, men and women, rich and poor, the young and their elders.

Moreover, as Tables 3-3 and 3-4 suggest, the composition of the 1968 convention delegations did not accurately reflect the composition of either the national electorate or party voters the same year. Both the electorate and the voters for Nixon and for Hum-

TABLE 3-3. *Characteristics of Total Population of the United States and of Persons Eligible to Vote, 1968*
Percent

Item	Total population	Persons eligible to vote[a]
Race[b]		
White	87.8	89.7
Non-white	12.1	10.3
Sex[b]		
Male	48.8	46.7
Female	51.1	53.3
Age[b]		
Under 25	46.4	10.0
25–34	11.8	19.9
35–44	11.7	19.7
45–54	11.4	19.4
55–64	8.9	15.2
65 and over	9.5	15.8
Annual family income[c]		
Under $5,000	22.4	24.9
$5,000–9,999	37.9	40.2
$10,000–14,999	25.0	19.0
$15,000 and over	14.7	9.3
Not reported	—	6.5

Note: Details may not add to 100 percent due to rounding.

a. Includes civilian noninstitutional population only. Adapted from U.S. Bureau of the Census data cited in Richard M. Scammon and Ben J. Wattenberg, *The Real Majority* (Coward, McCann & Geoghegan, 1970), pp. 343–44.

b. Race, sex, and age breakdowns of total population are estimates as of July 1, 1968. They include total resident population and exclude U.S. military personnel living abroad. U.S. Bureau of the Census, *Statistical Abstract of the United States: 1969* (Government Printing Office, 1969), p. 10.

c. Annual family income breakdown of total population is an estimate based on families as of March 1969. Military personnel included are only those living off the post or with family on the post. U.S. Bureau of the Census, *Statistical Abstract of the United States: 1971* (Government Printing Office, 1971), p. 316.

TABLE 3-4. *Characteristics of Presidential Voters, 1968: Percentage of Each Category Voting for the Democratic and Republican Tickets*

Item	Percentage voting Democratic	Percentage voting Republican
Race		
White	38	47
Non-white	85	12
Sex		
Male	41	43
Female	45	43
Age		
Under 30	47	38
31–49	44	41
50 and over	41	47
Occupation		
Professional/business	34	56
White collar	41	47
Manual workers	50	35
Farmers	29	51

Source: *Gallup Opinion Index,* Report No. 49 (July 1969), p. 29.
Note: Details do not add to 100 percent because Wallace voters are not included.

phrey included proportionately far more women, more non-whites, more young people and more elderly people, and more persons of modest incomes than were included in the convention delegations of either major party. All told, the delegates resembled political activists in their social characteristics more than rank-and-file partisans.[8]

This demographic pattern is unfair. If the political parties are quasi-public institutions, as is stated in Chapter 2, then they should reflect better their own constituencies. The major social characteristics of the delegations should more nearly correspond to those of the electorate and the party's own voters. This would require national party standards to ensure that, in particular, women, blacks, the young, the old, and the less affluent have a voice more

8. On the social characteristics of political activists, see Robert E. Lane, *Political Life: Why People Get Involved in Politics* (Free Press, 1959). Obviously the data in these three tables are not strictly comparable. But they are the best data available; and there is no question that blacks, women, the young, and the old were "underrepresented" at the 1968 conventions, as the term is used in this chapter.

appropriate to their numbers. Exactly how this change can be accomplished is a difficult question and will be considered later in this chapter.

Credentials Contests

Whatever the composition of the delegation, each state party typically has chosen and certified it in accordance with state law and its own rules; occasionally, however, the credentials of a slate certified by the state party have been contested, and the fireworks have begun. According to the most reliable estimates, only 4 percent of the delegate seats were contested at conventions between 1928 and 1956 and less than 10 percent from 1872 to 1956.[9] The 1968 Democratic convention had a record number of seating disputes, involving fifteen delegations.

Most of the credentials fights during the twentieth century have concerned the South. Before the Eisenhower era there were so few Republicans in many states of the old Confederacy that the party operated like a private club. At the 1912 convention, supporters of former President Theodore Roosevelt contested 176 southern delegates who backed President William Howard Taft, but they were unable to dislodge the incumbent chief executive from control of his party. The southern problem was eased at subsequent Republican conventions by new apportionment rules that gave the South proportionately fewer votes. (See Chapter 2.)

In 1952, the few long-time southern Republicans holding meetings at the local and state level in advance of the national convention suddenly found the meetings inundated with strangers. In many parts of the region where the Republican party had been in the hands of those sympathetic to the presidential candidacy of Ohio Senator Robert A. Taft, partisans of General Dwight D. Eisenhower emerged at public party gatherings to choose national convention delegates. The Taft supporters in some cases refused

9. Paul T. David, Ralph M. Goldman, and Richard C. Bain, *The Politics of National Party Conventions* (Brookings Institution, 1960), p. 263.

to recognize the newly arrived Eisenhower backers as real Republicans and withdrew to elect Taft delegates in closed caucuses. When formal conflicts between the factions arose at the state level, the Taft regulars on the state party committees tended to certify the delegates backing their candidate. Basically, the old-line southern Republicans in 1952 had state law and customs on their side; in many areas the concept of party affiliation was hazy at best, and a large proportion of the Eisenhower supporters were former Democrats.

But the Eisenhower faction at the national convention was able to maneuver a party decision based not on the past loyalty of the controversial delegations but rather on something few could oppose in principle: fair play. Senator Taft would have stood to gain if the contested southern delegates, who were supported by the Republican National Committee, were seated or even allowed to vote on the credentials committee report. Similar actions had enabled his father to win the credentials contests of 1912. This time, however, the Eisenhower group urged the adoption of a new rule prohibiting contested delegates from voting on credentials issues. The general's strategists devised, and shrewdly named, a "fair play" amendment to the convention rules, which provided that delegations supported by less than two-thirds of the national committee in its credentials deliberations should not be permitted to vote on any seating disputes. Taft backers argued that it was not fair to change the rules at the start of a major credentials battle. But the Eisenhower forces' slogan prevailed; after a floor fight, which was telecast to the nation, the amendment was adopted.

As a wistful Taft supporter put it, "Who can be against fair play?"[10] With momentum clearly on the Eisenhower side, the credentials committee held televised hearings; and in the glare of publicity the image shone brightly of the "fair play" supporters who had sought only to work for Eisenhower at open meetings, in contrast with the "anti-fair play" Taft side, which had sought to exclude Eisenhower people who called themselves Republicans

10. Quoted in Herbert Eaton, *Presidential Timber* (Free Press, 1964), p. 443.

from taking part in GOP gatherings. The Eisenhower forces won the credentials contests in Georgia, Louisiana, and Texas; their victory was clearly the turning point of the convention. The general went on to win the nomination on the first ballot and the November election in a landslide.

The Republican credentials battle of 1952 led to the adoption of new procedures for resolving such disputes. The fair play amendment indeed provided a more equitable arrangement than permitting all contested delegates to vote; but allowing delegates to vote who were supported by two-thirds of the national committee credentials panel hardly seems fair, for it permitted them to be among the judges in their own cases. In any event, in the aftermath of 1952 the Republicans also established a contest committee of the national committee to hold fact-finding hearings shortly before the convention. Delegates scheduled to be members of the convention credentials committee attend informally as observers. The contest committee's statement of facts is sent to the full national committee, which makes up the temporary roll. If delegates rejected for the temporary roll insist on their right to be seated, the credentials committee carries on its own deliberations, using the findings of the contest committee and holding additional hearings if necessary. The credentials panel draws up a permanent roll for the convention, including recommendations about contested seats, if any. The national convention itself is the final arbiter of who should be seated. By long-standing party rule, the seating of delegates is the first item of business at Republican conventions.

The South has provided an even more irksome credentials problem for the Democrats during the past two decades. Southern loyalty to the national ticket has been less than exemplary. Some prominent southern Democrats supported the States' Rights party in 1948, the Eisenhower ticket in 1952 and 1956, unpledged electors in 1960 and 1964, Barry Goldwater in the latter year, and George Wallace in 1968. Others simply sat at home. Accordingly, Democratic national conventions have become increasingly strict in their loyalty requirements. In 1952 every delegation was required as a precondition of being seated to assure the credentials committee that it would exert every effort to get electors who would support the convention nominees on the ballot under the Democratic emblem in their state. The official call for the 1956 national convention specifically stated the "understanding" that a state party in sending delegates to the national convention was in effect assuring that the nominees of that convention would be on the state ballot under the party label, that the certified delegates were bona fide Democrats, and that all members of the Democratic National Committee had the duty to support the national ticket at the peril of losing their seats if they failed to do so. Similar provisions were included in the calls for the 1960, 1964, and 1968 conventions. On this point, the 1972 call says:

> Be it resolved by the Democratic National Committee that:
> (1) It is the understanding that a State Democratic Party, in selecting and certifying delegates to the Democratic National Convention, thereby undertakes to assure that voters in the State . . . will have the opportunity to . . . cast their election ballots for the Presidential and Vice-Presidential nominees selected by . . . [the National] Convention, and for electors pledged formally and in good conscience to the election of these Presidential and Vice-Presidential nominees under the Democratic Party label and designation.[11]

In 1964, issues of fairness and democracy in the delegate selection process, foreshadowed by the earlier Republican controversy over fair play in credentials procedures, became manifest as the Mississippi Freedom Democratic party sent a predominantly Negro delegation to the Democratic national convention to challenge the all-white regular state party representatives. The dramatic climax of the credentials committee hearings, which were carried on national television, came as Fannie Lou Hamer, a black sharecropper's wife who had been fired from a Mississippi plantation job she had held for eighteen years on the day she sought to

---

11. Democratic National Committee, "Draft Final Call for the 1972 Democratic National Convention to be submitted to the Executive Committee of the Democratic National Committee on October 12, 1971" (processed), p. 1.

register to vote, told of how she had been forcibly denied access
to the deliberations of the Democratic party in her state:

> I was carried to the county jail. . . . After I was placed in the cell I
> began to hear sounds of licks and screams. . . .
>
> I was carried . . . into another cell where they had two Negro pris-
> oners. The State Highway Patrolmen ordered the first Negro to take
> the blackjack.
>
> The first Negro prisoner ordered me, by orders from the State
> Highway patrolman for me, to lay down on a bunk bed on my face,
> and I laid on my face.
>
> The first Negro began to beat, and I was beat . . . until he was ex-
> hausted. . . . After the first Negro . . . was exhausted, the State High-
> way Patrolman ordered the second Negro to take the blackjack. The
> second Negro began to beat . . . and the State Patrolman ordered the
> first Negro . . . to set on my feet. . . . I began to scream, and one white
> man got up and began to beat me in my head and tell me to hush. . . .
>
> All of this is on account we want to register, to become first-class
> citizens, and if the Freedom Democratic Party is not seated now, I
> question America. . . .[12]

Not only did the Freedom Democratic party charge that Negroes and whites opposed to racial segregation were systematically prohibited from participating in the regular Mississippi
party, sometimes by violent means; they also pointed out that the
Mississippi regulars had in the past bolted the presidential ticket
and platform of the national party, whereas the Freedom Democrats pledged their loyalty to President Lyndon B. Johnson and
his policies. Summing up the Freedom Democrats' case, their
counsel, Joseph L. Rauh, Jr., asked, "Are you going to throw out
of here the people who want to work for Lyndon Johnson, who
are willing to be beaten in jails for the privilege of working for
Lyndon Johnson?" Rhetorically he added, "Will the Democratic
party stand for the oppressors or for the oppressed?" The regular
Mississippi delegation denied the charges of discrimination and
emphasized that they had been legally selected by the procedures
established by the state party, under Mississippi law.

12. All quotations of participants are taken from an official stenotype transcript
of the credentials committee hearings on the Mississippi dispute.

Seeking to hold both the white South and the blacks, President Johnson decided that the regularly selected delegation should be seated in 1964 but pledged privately to the Freedom Democrats that their unhappy experiences would not be allowed to recur in 1968. The credentials committee announced a five-point solution. The Mississippi regulars would be seated if they signed a pledge to support the nominees of the convention. The Democratic National Committee was instructed to include in its call for the 1968 convention a requirement that in no state would race or any other ethnic or religious consideration be permitted to preclude opportunity for full participation by all Democrats in party affairs. A special equal rights committee of the national committee was to be established to ensure that this requirement was carried out. The Freedom Democrats' delegation was admitted to the 1964 convention as honored guests, and two of their leaders, Dr. Aaron E. Henry and the Reverend Edward King, were named as delegates-at-large to the whole convention. Eventually, twenty-one other Freedom Democrats obtained access to the convention floor, reputedly with credentials from other delegations and reporters. Defying attempts to remove them from the hall, they sat in the Mississippi seats left empty when all but four of the regulars left the convention.

The promise to the Freedom Democrats was kept in 1968. An integrated delegation, the Loyal Democrats of Mississippi, successfully contested the regulars and was subsequently recognized by the Democratic National Committee as the official party in that state. Fannie Lou Hamer was a member of the delegation that was seated. An integrated Georgia delegation, consisting half of regulars and half of challengers who had claimed exclusion on racial grounds, also was seated in 1968.

The principle of democracy in the delegate selection process was extended far beyond the realm of racial discrimination at the 1968 Democratic convention in wide-ranging challenges to allegedly unfair selection procedures. Though largely unsuccessful in 1968, these contests paved the way for party inquiries into the delegate selection process and credentials systems. As a result of the contests, the 1968 convention voted to ban the use of the unit rule at all levels of the party and to ensure open delegate selection procedures in 1972.

Under that mandate, the Commission on Rules and the Commission on Party Structure and Delegate Selection were established. The former panel considered various credentials procedures in drafting formal regulations for the 1972 convention. Previously, credentials disputes (like other matters) had been governed only by precedent; in substance, they had been resolved in a system corresponding to the Republican method. The new rules for 1972 formally established a credentials panel within the national committee, required strict legal procedures for filing and responding to credentials challenges, authorized impartial fact-finding hearing officers, and adopted an elaborate set of rules for credentials committee deliberations and reports that were to be made available to all delegates at least forty-eight hours before the opening of the convention. As in past practice, delegates on the temporary roll were prohibited from voting in any contest for their own seats. Since the credentials committee report was made the first order of business, the contested delegates would not vote on other important matters unless the convention approved a special order of business that involved considering some other measure first. In all, the new Democratic rules were inherently fair; they required only fair administration, which, of course, no written set of regulations can ensure.

Alternative Standards for Delegate Selection

Since the parties have adopted new procedures for resolving credentials disputes—the Republicans after 1952 and the Democrats after 1968—little controversy has remained about the arrangements for resolving seating contests. In contrast, questions of delegate selection have remained highly controversial.

WHAT THE PARTIES HAVE DONE

After the 1968 election, both national parties established groups to study delegate selection—the Democrats a Commission on Party Structure and Delegate Selection and the Republicans a Delegates and Organizations (DO) Committee. The mandates of the two panels were different. The Democrats' commission was created to fulfill a resolution of the convention that "all feasible efforts [be] made to assure that delegates are selected through party primary, convention, or committee procedures open to public participation within the calendar year of the national convention."[13] This meant requiring an emphasis on more opportunity for influence by rank-and-file Democrats and, by inference, less authority for established leaders. The Republicans' DO Committee was authorized by a rule approved at their 1968 convention, which instructed the Republican National Committee to appoint a group to study the relationships among various GOP organizations, as well as implementation of a new rule, also adopted in 1968, forbidding discrimination on the basis of race, religion, color, or national origin in the Republican delegate selection process.[14] Their task then was to make recommendations dealing with discrimination on demographic grounds, rather than with the promotion of wide public participation.

The Democratic commission set up eighteen guidelines requiring adoption by the state parties of explicit written rules on delegate selection to guarantee certain procedural safeguards for fair deliberation, to open party meetings to all interested Democrats, and to make other changes in the delegate selection process. The procedural safeguards (1) ban proxy voting and the unit rule, (2) remove all mandatory assessments of the national convention dele-

13. Quoted in Democratic National Committee, Commission on Party Structure and Delegate Selection, *Mandate for Reform* (1970), p. 15.

14. Republican National Committee, Delegates and Organizations Committee, Progress Report, Part II, *The Delegate Selection Procedures for the Republican Party* (1971), p. 4.

gation and limit required fees to no more than $10 and delegate petition requirements to no more than 1 percent of the state's Democratic voters, (3) ensure that all party meetings outside rural areas are held on uniform dates in easily accessible public places, and (4) require adequate public notice of all official meetings concerning the selection of national convention delegates. The guidelines, which aimed at a broader participatory base for the party, specifically added the antidiscrimination rules of the Democratic National Committee[15] to state party rules; required the state parties to "encourage" minority-group, young, and women delegates "in reasonable relationship"[16] to their percentage of the state's population; and authorized all persons at least eighteen years old to take part in all party affairs. They made no mention of the elderly, who were also underrepresented at the 1968 convention in terms of their percentage of the electorate and of party voters. Finally, the guidelines also required the state parties to choose alternates in the same manner as delegates, ban ex officio delegates, carry out the entire delegate selection process during the calendar year of the national convention, select at least 75 percent of state convention delegates at a level no higher than the congressional district and follow apportionment formulas for state conventions based on population and party voting, designate fully and publicly the procedures by which delegate slates are prepared and may be challenged, and choose no more than 10 percent of their national convention delegates by any state party committee.

In addition to its *requirements* for the state parties, the Commis-

---

15. The national committee's antidiscrimination standards, adopted in 1966, provided that all public party meetings should be open to all Democrats; that no tests of party membership would be permitted that required support for racial, religious, or ethnic discrimination; that all public party meetings should be well publicized and held in convenient locations with adequate facilities for large attendance; that the party at all levels should support a maximum voter registration effort; that state parties should fully publicize well in advance the process by which all the various party officers and representatives would be chosen; and that all state parties should broadcast fully and widely the qualifications for such offices so that all prospective candidates would have an adequate chance to compete for them.

16. Democratic National Committee, *Mandate for Reform*, p. 40.

sion on Party Structure and Delegate Selection also *urged* them to
take further actions. These included eliminating all costs and fees
in delegate selection, exploring ways to ease financial strain on
those seeking to participate in the national convention, removing
restrictive registration and voting procedures, providing easy access and frequent opportunity for non-Democrats to become party
members, ending the appointment system of naming delegates, and
providing fair representation of minority candidate factions in
delegate selection.

All the Democratic guidelines aimed explicitly at opening up
the delegate selection process to rank-and-file participation and at
discouraging autonomous control by party leaders. Taken all together, the guidelines also facilitated the efforts of political insurgents and other often-excluded groups—blacks, other ethnic minorities, the young, and women. They would also help the candidacy
of anyone strongly supported by such groups—in 1972, perhaps
George McGovern or John Lindsay or Shirley Chisholm—and
work against anyone unpopular with the groups. Although the
guidelines may be amended after 1972, their influence will be
permanent as precedents for national party standards and requirements for wide participation.

With a President in the White House planning to run again,
with less intraparty controversy over delegate selection, and with
a more limited mandate, the Republican DO Committee report
made ten recommendations to the national committee for its consideration in contemplating new rules that would be voted on by
the 1972 convention for use in 1976. Many of the recommendations of the Democratic panel were not needed in the Republican
party. Republican rules have long been more formal than those of
the Democrats; the unit rule has been used very rarely by the Republicans, and it has never been enforced at national conventions;
no GOP delegates may be selected before the call is issued early in
the presidential election year; and fewer Republican delegates
have been selected by party committees. Like its Democratic
counterpart, however, the DO Committee recommended banning

proxy voting, ending required assessments of delegates and alternates, selecting alternates in the same manner as delegates, and prohibiting ex officio delegates. In recommendations similar to the Democratic guidelines, the DO Committee urged open local meetings for all qualified citizens in states that have conventions, an attempt by each state to have equal representation of men and women in its national convention delegation, and inclusion of delegates under twenty-five years of age in proportion to their voting strength in each state. In addition, the DO Committee called for consideration of holding district and state conventions on different days in different communities, in order to widen participation; and assistance by the Republican National Committee in informing all citizens about how to take part in delegate selection. Finally, in its most controversial recommendation, the DO Committee suggested amending the written national convention rules to require each state delegation to select one man, one woman, one delegate under twenty-five years of age, and one member of a minority ethnic group as its four members on each of the four convention committees. Like the Democratic guidelines, they did not recommend more representation for the elderly, who in 1968 were proportionately more numerous at the Republican than at the Democratic convention.

While few would quarrel with most of the recommendations made by the DO Committee, on the whole they did not go as far as the Democratic guidelines. They did not touch upon the structure and operations of state conventions, slatemaking bodies, appointment of delegates by party committees, voter registration, party enrollment, and representation for minority candidate factions, all of which were covered by the Democratic standards. Hence, while they would eliminate some practices considered to be unfair, and some that have inhibited participation by specific groups, the DO Committee recommendations would have little effect on which presidential candidates won and lost, attempts by insurgents to dislodge established leaders, and so on. If its recommendations are adopted, the consequences of the DO Committee report will be felt less in selection procedures than in the *sociological composition* of the delegations at the national convention.

IMPLICATIONS OF WIDENED PARTICIPATION

The timely, open, broadly based delegate selection procedures required by the Democratic guidelines (and largely implied by the DO Committee effort) are fair, democratic, and wholly commendable; their weakness is their uncertain implications for an accurate reflection of rank-and-file candidate preferences. The McGovern-Fraser Commission decided, probably correctly, that its mandate from the 1968 convention did not include a guarantee of fair representation for candidate factions. It did forbid the unit rule and require that any state using the convention system select at least 75 percent of its total delegation at a level no higher than that of the congressional district, and it urged the state parties to provide fair representation for all presidential candidates.

In order to be fair and democratic as the terms are used in this book, national delegate selection standards should require the national convention delegation from states with a presidential primary to reflect the outcome of that contest. Thus, in states with a winner-take-all primary, the entire delegate slate of the presidential candidate who received the most popular votes should be elected. In states with a congressional district selection system and a primary, the delegates on the slates of the candidates who win at large and in each district should be elected. Some states might prefer to divide their votes in proportion to each presidential candidate's showing in the primary. In states using the appointment and convention systems, national standards should require party officials charged with selecting the delegates to be governed by the preferences of the state's party voters, as best they can be ascertained.

Ironically, wide public participation—instead of being divisive and destructive of party organization as has long been feared—may have the reverse effect. Now that the standards of democracy and fairness in delegate selection have been raised, the presidential

candidates who are disadvantaged by unfair procedures will not
hesitate to challenge credentials. Always seeking a good story, the
news media will broadcast the particulars fully. Thus party unity
would be endangered by disputes that are based on charges of unfairness in delegate selection. If there were no unfairness, there
would be no challenges on those grounds, except for frivolous
contests. Because the issues involved would be more technical, the
disputes would be less disruptive of the party in its national convention and the ensuing campaign.

DEMOGRAPHIC REPRESENTATION

Newly intensified claims for increased political representation
by blacks, other ethnic groups, the young, and women have made
it inevitable that any review of political conventions consider the
demographic composition of their membership. The delegate selection panels of both parties have sought to include more representatives of these previously underrepresented groups in the state
delegations. The DO Committee recommended such a change
without a significant increase in the overall number of delegates
(although the size of convention committees would be doubled);
hence the new Republican delegates presumably would get seats
at the expense of male long-time party workers, contributors, and
other GOP activists. The Democrats, however, increased the number of convention votes from 2,622 in 1968 to 3,016 in 1972, with
the number of delegates somewhat higher because of some fractional voting. This has relieved somewhat the competitive pressure
for seats between the newly included groups and the old-line party
faithful; but the increase in size has other, less felicitous, implications that are described in Chapter 4; and in any case the new
groups have assessed their strength in terms of percentages rather
than of numbers alone.

Beyond their agreement on broadened demographic representation, the parties have had differing emphases. While in both parties the thrust is toward approximately equal representation for
women, the Republican panel stressed this factor in the individual
state delegations only; they required that only one of each state's

four representatives on convention committees be a woman, instead of one out of two as at present. The Democratic guidelines urge that women delegates be chosen in "reasonable relationship" to their share of each state's population, and the new Democratic rules call for the states to select equal or nearly equal numbers of men and women as members of the convention committees.

The Democratic reformers have been more oriented than the Republicans toward the black community, which since the New Deal era has been overwhelmingly Democratic. While its guidelines covered all minority groups, the report of the Democrats' delegate selection commission specifically noted the paucity of black delegates in 1968; many of the restrictive practices whose abolition it recommended were registration and enrollment procedures often used in the South to deny the franchise to Negroes. In contrast, the DO Committee report referred to members of all minority ethnic groups and did not ban any specific practices that served as barriers to black participation.

Similarly, although both parties urged easing the financial strain on delegates and alternates, the Democrats made more recommendations intended to help the less affluent, who are predominantly Democratic. They urged fewer costs for all participating in delegate selection. Their call for an end to literacy tests and similar practices also aimed at more participation by poorer persons.

While almost no one would dispute the objectives of these measures to assure representation for previously underrepresented groups, they entail insoluble paradoxes in the idea of representation. At any political level, it is impossible to ensure that the convention delegation simultaneously will reflect the presidential preferences of the party rank-and-file and be a perfect microcosm of the state's population or of its party voters. The nearest approximation would be to name a demographically representative slate and bind the delegates to abide by the results of a separate presidential preference primary. That would work, however, only if the presidential nominee could be selected on the first ballot. Otherwise, in order to reach a consensus, the delegates would have to be released from the candidate preferences of the voters.

Demographic demands also may clash with the objective of wide participation. In order to achieve descriptive representation[17] of social groups, each state party would have to draw up a balanced ticket of delegates; but this would violate the principle of broad participation by ordinary partisans in delegate selection.

A balanced ticket also would mean the use of quotas, which are inherently restrictive, and would emphasize demographic considerations at the expense of such reasonable criteria as merit and experience. In addition, quotas raise the specter of an infinite regression of representation of every conceivable group that has developed political consciousness. Clearly the line must be drawn somewhere. There is no need for there to be as great a percentage of persons under 18 among delegates to conventions as there are in the total population; probably there need not be as great a percentage over 65 either, although there should be more than there were at the 1968 Democratic convention. Similarly, the interests of poor farmers may be represented well by a delegate employed by the National Farmers' Union who makes $20,000 a year; but there should be more poor people representing themselves. Exact descriptive representation of every group is neither possible nor desirable. Reasonable representation of salient groups is a more appropriate criterion.

Finally, past experience is chastening. After women received the vote in 1920, they were added in numbers equal to men on many party units, including the national committees; but in most cases the men kept the power, and the women merely served as figureheads. Political equality for women—or for blacks, the young, or anyone else—will not be obtained simply by allotting some hypothetical ratios to these groups. Yet mandatory equality is an important first step if these groups are to have a fair share in presidential politics. Those who seek to avoid the fate of the women's movement after 1920 should make every effort to ensure that the women, blacks, youth, aged, poor, and so on who *do* become convention delegates are able representatives of their groups.

17. See Hanna Pitkin, *The Concept of Representation* (University of California Press, 1967), Chap. 4.

Desirable as it is that more political recognition be accorded to these groups, the central issue of democracy in the delegate selection process must be the extent of rank-and-file influence in terms of candidate preference. The best way would be for the candidates or their organizations to select delegate slates that are demographically representative, and for state and local officials to be required by national standards to provide for delegations that are representative of candidate factions and of demographic groups—in that order. It is not an easy task to carry out; but it is necessary if delegate selection is to be fair and democratic.

LOYALTY REQUIREMENTS

Another kind of national standard for delegate selection is the assurance that those chosen will aid the party's ticket in their states. National Democratic party leaders actually backed into the subject of delegate selection standards by requiring assurances that delegates would work at least to get the convention's nominees on the ballot back home. That requirement became a standard part of the convention call during the 1950s. Making loyalty to the national ticket a precondition of delegate status was an opening wedge in the increasing scrutiny of delegate credentials.

Some observers have argued that a loyalty oath should be the only national party standard enforced on convention delegates. Delving any further into the states' delegate selection processes, they have contended, represents arbitrary interference with the representation of the state parties:

> After delegate election and a failure or absence of court challenge, the duty of the convention in delegate certification becomes ministerial, with the exception of holding delegates to party loyalty. The convention's sole duty is to carry out the mandate of state party members expressed in the exercise of the voting franchise.[18]

Significantly, the quotation comes from a recent article in the *Georgia Law Review*.

18. "Selecting and Certifying National Political Convention Delegates—a Party or a State Right?" *Georgia Law Review*, Vol. 4 (Winter 1970), p. 894.

The Republicans have allowed even more leeway to the state parties in that there have been no national loyalty requirements for delegates at Republican conventions. The principal reason has been that the GOP has not had the substantial, continuing problem with a potentially rebellious section that the Democrats have had with the South. The Republican national ticket has not been kept off a state ballot as the Democratic ticket has on some occasions. Equally significant has been the Republican faith in the legitimacy of their state and local delegate selection processes. Delegates who have been duly chosen through regular processes of their area's party without protest at that level are accepted as bona fide Republicans, the vast majority of whom will faithfully support the party ticket.

In contrast, the Democrats have added a far more stringent loyalty requirement to the convention call for 1972. In addition to the usual language designed to get the national Democratic ticket on the ballot everywhere, the call to the convention expresses the further understanding that the state parties will assure that the delegates they certify will not publicly support or campaign for any other presidential ticket. The new language is intended to prevent or inhibit participation in Democratic presidential politics both by southern (and northern) supporters of Alabama Governor George Wallace and by that Democratic faction that is prepared to support a left-wing minor-party ticket if the Democratic candidates are not to its liking. The latter group has complained bitterly that the new rule is unfair, since such sanctions have not been applied to many disloyal southerners in the past. Yet since 1964 the unreconstructed southerners effectively have been excluded from Democratic presidential politics on loyalty grounds. The new rule is fair in that it is applied equally. And it is as reasonable as the idea of party loyalty itself.

JUDICIAL REGULATION

Another means of establishing national standards of delegate selection is through the court system. This approach is not a strict alternative to the activities of the parties themselves but a possible avenue if the parties' efforts should prove inadequate.

Because judges are still wary of what Felix Frankfurter called "the political thicket," the extent of the courts' jurisdiction over political parties is a troubled question of constitutional law. With respect to the national party conventions, judicial regulation would have some advantages and some shortcomings.

Supporters of judicial regulation[19] base their case on the doctrine of equal protection of the laws, guaranteed by the Fourteenth Amendment to the Constitution. Thus, they contend, the process of selecting national convention delegates must be reconcilable with the Supreme Court's one-person-one-vote standard. Any process that was based on malapportionment of electoral districts or jurisdictions from which representatives to local and state conventions were chosen would be clearly unconstitutional under this standard. Moreover, any system of delegate selection by a party elite would be patently a denial of equal protection because most citizens would have no opportunity to participate in their party's deliberations.

If the courts found a particular delegate controversy to be a justiciable issue and intervened in delegate selection, they could set up some general standards of public participation that applied to all parties at all levels. For those who believed themselves aggrieved, there would be the possibility of remedy through a lawsuit rather than through the vagaries of internal party politics. A court decision probably would be accepted by many concerned as more legitimate than a decision reached by party officials. It probably would be less affected by its implications for various presidential candidates.

And yet judicial regulation would have its drawbacks. While clearly the courts could prevent inequities like malapportionment and racial or sex discrimination, it is more difficult to see how the equal protection clause could be stretched to cover timeliness and

19. See "Constitutional Safeguards in the Selection of Delegates to Presidential Nominating Conventions," *Yale Law Journal*, Vol. 78 (June 1969), pp. 1228–52.

perhaps other areas of concern that are dealt with, for example, in the Democratic guidelines. Even if the equal protection doctrine were extended to include most of the points in the guidelines, it is unlikely that the change would be as rapid as the change that has come about—recently, at least—through the mechanism of the political party. The Supreme Court of the 1970s is unlikely to intervene in party affairs. The court system also may be insufficiently responsive to resolve a given complaint before it is rendered moot by the onrush of events. Administratively, it is more feasible to settle credentials conflicts at a party gathering than in the already massively overburdened courts. Judicial regulation should be viewed as a last resort in attempts to achieve fairness and democracy in delegate selection.

On the whole, delegate selection is a subject that requires active efforts to ensure fairness and democracy. One way is to require appropriate procedures in the institutions that select the delegates so that the men and women chosen represent the candidate preferences of their constituencies. Another approach is to make certain that a fair number of the politically emerging groups become delegates. A third method is to assure that the process for settling disputes over credentials is itself fair, as well as an efficient means of protecting fairness and democracy in delegate selection. To these ends, national party standards aimed at wide public participation, demographic representation, and party loyalty are required; and judicial regulation may also be needed. Some principles may tend to conflict, but they can be made complementary. They must be made to work.

Chapter Four

☆

FAIRNESS, DEMOCRACY, AND DELIBERATION

It is clear that how things are done in an organization or an institution may affect what is done.
Lewis A. Froman, Jr.

THE OPEN CONVENTION, making decisions unbossed by party leaders and responsive to the popular will, is the ideal of the contemporary reform movement. If a convention is fair and democratic, it will have a structure and procedures that are appropriate to those ends. This means not only that the methods for selecting delegates meet such standards but also that the convention itself as an assembly is fairly constituted and run, under widely accepted rules. These conditions facilitate the making of decisions that fairly represent the views of the delegates' constituencies.

In a sense, these qualities are not always needed, since at many conventions major decisions are a foregone conclusion. Such conventions are ratifying rather than deliberative bodies. Nonetheless, fairness and democracy are necessary for those occasions when a convention must make decisions; and as a matter of principle they ought to obtain at the ratifying conventions as well.

The Character of Convention Deliberation

Recent discussion of this subject typically has begun with a false dichotomy. Both right-wing Republicans and left-wing Democrats have charged that their respective parties' conventions were controlled by a party elite, presumably at the expense of the mass of delegates and/or party adherents throughout the country. Until 1964, Republican conservatives had long complained about control by the "Eastern Establishment" over GOP presidential nominations. Left-wing Democrats, in 1968 and thereafter, criticized the "power structure" in Chicago and Washington; they expressed their aspirations in such phrases as "the convention belongs to the delegates."[1]

Actually, the nature of decision-making at conventions is much more complicated than the situation symbolized by the use of the terms "elite" and "mass." Past conventions have operated through bargaining among various leaders and between leaders and their constituencies. Although all concerned want the convention to make its decisions and get on with the campaign, there are many different interests. Presidential candidates and their managers follow Sam Rayburn's dictum that in order to become a statesman you must first be elected. They are interested primarily in winning the nomination and the election; accordingly, they view all convention decisions from that perspective. They may want an efficient, harmonious convention, with a platform that will appeal to as many segments of the voters as possible, if that will help them win; but above all they want to win. Convention officers and officials also want their party to win, but their own first priority is a smoothly running convention, for that is their responsibility. State

1. A quotation from the playwright Arthur Miller, a McCarthy delegate in 1968, indicates that their complaints were based on frustrating personal experience rather than conceptual sophistication:

The McCarthy people had been warned not to bring posters into the hall, but at the first mention from the platform of Hubert Humphrey's name hundreds of 3-by-5-foot Humphrey color photos broke out all over the place. By the third day I could not converse with anybody except by sitting down; a standing conversation would bring inspectors, sometimes every 15 seconds, asking for my credentials and those of anyone talking to me. . . . And the ultimate mocking of the credentials themselves was the flooding of the balconies by Daley ward heelers who carried press passes.

"The Battle of Chicago: From the Delegates' Side," *New York Times Magazine*, Sept. 15, 1968, pp. 30–31.

delegation leaders want their party to win and want to reap the political benefits of having supported the winner at the convention, but they are concerned primarily with the politics of their own delegations. A national convention takes place for a few days every four years; most of the time these delegation leaders are state politicians. They seek to make bargains within and for their own delegations that will consolidate their position of leadership. This process may take a number of forms because the factional situation in state delegations may vary from virtual unanimity to serious disagreement. Similarly, leaders of such party factions as organized labor, southern Democrats, and conservative Republicans all are seeking bargains that will do the most for their groups and thereby enhance their own positions.

Satisfaction with the nature of the bargaining has varied in the past with the overall strategic situation. When an incumbent President has been standing for reelection or designating a successor, he fundamentally has controlled the convention; but the vast majority of delegates has readily gone along with his wishes and has found little or nothing unfair about doing so. When, however, there has been a major battle for the presidential nomination, the convention has been more nearly democratic and deliberative in the sense that no single person's wishes have dominated it; but in these cases delegates supporting candidates other than the front-runner have been more discontented and more inclined to criticize the fairness of convention procedures.

Each leader's bargaining position has depended on the relationship of the leader to his or her particular constituency and on whether the constituents were insistent or compliant about the issue involved. Some leaders have been governed by the inclinations of their constituencies; others have acted more independently. If the constituency has been indifferent about a pending question, the leader has had more freedom to maneuver; if it has felt very strongly about a matter, the leader has had little choice but to hold out for whatever the constituency wanted. Thus, if a state delegation or the black community or the labor unions or big business has taken a very firm position on a platform issue or a prospective vice presidential nominee or any other question, their leaders might have persisted in the viewpoint whatever the position of the convention officials or of various presidential candidates or even of the President.

Finally, the kind of bargaining that has taken place has been shaped by the formal rules and procedures for setting up and operating the convention. Thus, reforms that are being made in delegate selection procedures, particularly in the Democratic party, will change the nature of the bargaining among leaders at the 1972 conventions. Minority candidate factions within the states will have a greater share of the delegates under the Democratic provision that in states that have conventions at least 75 percent must be selected at a level no higher than the congressional district. With the unit rule abolished, with these national convention delegations more divided as to candidate preference, and with more delegates elected in primaries and bound, or at least committed, to particular presidential candidates, the candidate organizations will have relatively stronger bargaining positions; and state delegation leaders will have correspondingly weaker positions at national conventions. Accordingly, the major concerns of the candidates will assume greater importance—and those of the state delegation leaders will be less important—in convention deliberations.

Because there will be more opportunity for a broader spread of candidate preferences, reaching a decision may be accomplished less readily at such a convention. It will be less easy for the front-runner to capture the nomination quickly. Further, the new system seems likely to produce a greater number of issue-oriented "amateur" delegates. Many experienced state and local leaders who are skilled politicians and well known in their areas will continue to be selected as delegates. But in other cases, issue-oriented opponents will be able to persuade the voters (and the politicians who listen to them) that some old-line activists should be replaced. The "amateurs" are concerned with intraparty democracy and are less willing than are the more traditional delegates to compromise for the sake of party unity.[2] If there were a threat of a protracted division at a convention, much would depend on the willingness of the presidential contenders themselves to reach agreement and on their capacity to persuade their supporters among the delegates to accept the decision.

Thus the new rules for the convention will mean more old-fashioned bargaining. Issues of fairness and democracy concern the *kind* of bargaining that takes place. In a realistically open and democratic convention, the rules would apply equally to all and would not discriminate regularly against anyone. Each delegate would be free to vote for whomever he or she chose. Each vote would count equally, and the candidate with a majority would win and would assume control over the party. Within those conditions, an enormous variety of politicking is both permissible and inevitable.

One unresolved question of deliberation at an open convention—a gathering that is fair and democratic rather than governed by a closed elite—concerns the relationship between the delegates and their constituencies. An open convention could mean that all the delegates were pledged to carry out the wishes of the rank-and-file partisans to whom they were responsible; with equal plausibility, it could mean that all the delegates were unpledged and autonomous actors, free to vote their own consciences. The mandate–independence controversy is one of the great insoluble dilemmas in the theory of representative government.[3] Although both situations fall within the meaning of the open convention, the political orientations of the two would be quite different—one facing homeward and the other focused within the convention hall. In a divided convention, agreement and decision could come readily if all delegates were unpledged, but not if all were indefi-

---

2. See John W. Soule and James W. Clarke, "Amateurs and Professionals: A Study of Delegates to the 1968 Democratic National Convention," *American Political Science Review*, Vol. 64 (September 1970), p. 896.

3. See Hanna F. Pitkin, *The Concept of Representation* (University of California Press, 1967), Chap. 7.

nitely bound to the will of their constituents. Thus, it is more reasonable for delegates to be selected on the basis of a firm commitment to a particular candidate and viewpoint rather than of the requirement that they are *bound* to that candidate for a particular number of ballots.

Beyond these general requirements, specific rules for the convention shape the nature of the bargaining that takes place. Some rules more than others are conducive to rational deliberation under fair and democratic conditions.

Size and Deliberation

"Had every Athenian citizen been a Socrates," James Madison wrote, "every Athenian assembly would still have been a mob"[4]—because it had too many participants. At presidential nominating conventions—with several thousand delegates, alternates, staff members, reporters, camera crews, gate crashers, and others jammed into the hall—the average television viewer may have a better idea than they of what is going on. Indeed, many delegates and others at the convention watch television to learn what is happening. In such an environment, the participants themselves—the delegates—have a tendency to feel lost and ineffectual. "What can I do?" was the plaintive question of one of the 82-member Ohio delegation to the 1960 Democratic convention.[5] By the same token, the officials of such a gathering tend to assume greater control over its formal actions; someone must lead, and in the confusion it is difficult for anyone to challenge the officials' decisions successfully. Very large size, in short, does little to foster the capability of the convention as a decision-making or even a decision-ratifying body.

Recent conventions have been very large; Democratic conven-

4. Jacob E. Cooke (ed.), *The Federalist* (Wesleyan University Press, 1961), Paper No. 55, p. 374.
5. Aaron B. Wildavsky, " 'What Can I Do?' Ohio Delegates View the Democratic Convention," in Paul Tillett (ed.), *Inside Politics: The National Conventions, 1960* (Oceana, 1962), pp. 112–31.

tions in particular have grown enormously. Table 4-1 shows the number of delegates and alternates at the major party conventions from 1952 through 1968. For 1972 there will be 1,347 delegates and 1,347 alternates at the Republican convention. Total votes at the Democratic convention were set at 3,016 in the apportionment formula approved by the Democratic National Committee (see Chapter 2). Because of fractional voting in small delegations, there will be 3,103 Democratic delegates. There will be 1,897 alternates, apportioned on the basis of state delegation size.

TABLE 4-1. *Numbers of Delegates and Alternates at the Major Party National Conventions, 1952–68*

	Democrats[a]		Republicans[b]	
Year	Delegates	Alternates	Delegates	Alternates
1952	1,639	1,617	1,206	1,206
1956	2,483	1,830	1,323	1,323
1960	2,716	1,490	1,331	1,331
1964	2,927	2,106	1,308	1,308
1968	3,057	2,453	1,333	1,333

a. Based on unofficial delegate lists in official convention proceedings (1952–64) and in *The Presidential Nominating Conventions, 1968* (Congressional Quarterly Service, 1968), pp. 243–78.

b. Republican National Committee, Delegates and Organizations Committee, *Progress Report, Part II, The Delegate Selection Procedures for the Republican Party* (1971), p. 93.

The gargantuan size of Democratic conventions is a very recent development. Between 1932 and 1960, Democratic conventions ran between 1,100 and slightly more than 1,500 votes; the median was 1,236 votes. But with the new apportionment rules approved (see Chapter 2), the 1964 convention totaled 2,295 votes; as a result of President Johnson's overwhelming victory in 1964, the 1968 convention had 2,622 votes. Fractional voting resulted in the even greater number of delegates reflected in Table 4-1. In contrast, Republican conventions remained at about the same size from 1952 through 1968, increasing only slightly with the growth of the party in the South and in the population as a whole.[6]

6. William J. Crotty, "Size of the Convention and Apportionment of Delegates," Democratic National Committee (July 1970; processed), pp. 3–4.

Though the ranks of convention participants have grown since 1952, particularly at Democratic gatherings, the number of additional people on the scene has grown even more. In 1968 the Republican National Committee planned to accommodate 7,000 representatives of the news media alone. There is no way of knowing the exact number of messengers, honored guests, relatives of delegates and alternates, security guards, staff members, lobbyists, non-journalists with press credentials, military surveillance operatives, and others who found their way into the hall; but the number was substantial in both parties. Convention veterans readily agree that the number of non-participants attending far outstripped the number of delegates and alternates. In order to accommodate them, the 1968 Republican site selection committee listed as criteria for selecting a convention city "at least 14,000 seats in the convention hall" and "at least 10,000 first-class hotel rooms within a reasonable radius of the convention center."[7]

While size is a relative matter, the national conventions are clearly enormous assemblies. Yet one easily could argue that this does not affect the decision-making process substantially, since the important decisions long since have been shifted to smaller arenas —the convention committees and the individual state delegations. But the size of these bodies too is large and growing.

The typical state delegation at the 1972 conventions will hardly be an intimate group. All Republican delegations will have one delegate and one alternate for each convention vote. The exact size of Democratic delegations is a more complex matter. Each state gets one delegate for each of its votes, except that states (and the District of Columbia) with fewer than 20 votes may send up to 20 delegates to cast them. The Canal Zone, Guam, and the Virgin Islands get 3 votes each and may send as many as 6 delegates each; Puerto Rico gets 7 votes and may send up to 14 delegates. Alternates are assigned to each jurisdiction on the bases of one alternate for each of the first 20 convention votes, plus one alternate for

7. Republican National Committee, "Report of the Committee on the Selection of the Site for the 1968 Republican National Convention" (processed), p. 1.

each 2 votes over 20 but less than 101, plus one alternate for each 3 votes over 100.

The median Republican state delegation in 1972 will have 20 delegates and 20 alternates. The median Democratic state delegation will have 35 delegates and 28 alternates. Five Republican delegations and twenty Democratic delegations will have 50 or more delegates plus a complement of alternates in 1972. Nine Democratic delegations will have over 100 delegates, plus alternates. The largest state delegation, the New York Democratic delegation, has been apportioned 278 delegates and 120 alternates. This group of 398 approaches the size of the United States House of Representatives—a body that many believe is able to function despite its great size only because of very strict procedural rules, widespread internal consensus based on long tenure and common experience, and a low rate of turnover among the members. National convention rules, and certainly informal state delegation rules, are far less strict; and usually more than half the delegates are attending for the first time.[8] Only in the smaller state delegations are effective discussion and deliberation possible. By sheer necessity, the state delegation chairmen must assume control of the larger groupings.

Convention committees also have been relatively large groups and apparently will become larger. Through 1968, each committee consisted typically of one man and one woman from each state and territorial delegation. If there were not enough women in a delegation to make this possible, the Democrats permitted a second man to serve; the Republicans instead allowed only one member from that state. The result was committees in each party of slightly over 100 members.

When the Democrats were considering changes in their convention rules in 1969, Paul T. David urged them to restructure the standing committees and reduce their size. He suggested committees with a maximum of 40 members, selected in the same way

8. Loch K. Johnson and Harlan Hahn, "Turnover at the National Party Conventions, 1944–1968" (unpublished manuscript).

members of congressional committees are chosen—by a committee on committees composed of state delegation chairmen who would meet several weeks prior to the convention. Geography, sex, race, and experience would be among the criteria for selection. Committee members would no longer specifically represent their states, although the group of leaders selecting them would be apportioned on a territorial basis. In David's opinion, reducing the size of committees—like reducing convention size—would facilitate better deliberation. It would also make the convention less confederal and more national in structure and emphasis.[9] Deliberation about any such recommendation should include careful consideration of the composition of the new committee on committees.

For 1972, however, the Democrats' O'Hara Commission on Rules has taken the opposite course and has recommended committees of up to 150 members, apportioned by the national committee "in accordance with the state's delegation size,"[10] including at least one delegate from each state and territory. Thus the bases of the apportionment of votes in the full convention—including party voting and population as well as sovereignty—will be the bases of committee vote apportionment. The committees also will be about 50 percent larger than in the past. The change shows the head-on clash between the principles of representativeness and of efficient deliberation.

Republican reformers have moved still further to increase committee size in order to increase representativeness. Their Delegates and Organizations (DO) Committee has recommended that the 1972 convention approve a rule for 1976 whereby each state delegation would be required to select one man, one woman, one delegate under the age of twenty-five, and one "member of a mi-

9. Paul T. David, statement before the Commission on Rules, Democratic National Committee, May 17, 1969 (processed), pp. 13–14.

10. Democratic National Committee, Commission on Rules, "Determinations of the Commission on Rules with Respect to the National Nominating Convention" (1971; processed), pp. 3, 5, 12; reprinted in *Congressional Record*, daily ed., Oct. 21, 1971, pp. E11182–87.

nority ethnic group"[11] to serve on each of the convention committees. This would mean that every committee would have over 200 members, a 100 percent increase in size. While the larger committees would be more representative because they would include more young people and a broader ethnic mix, they would be apportioned not in the same way as the full convention, but instead on the old basis of territorial sovereignty alone.

Thus, on issues of size, the parties have moved away from improving their capacity for decision-making. Certainly the size of conventions and their principal constituent units is too large to be conducive to serious deliberation, particularly in the Democratic party. Despite wide consensus on that point, the prospects are dim for a reduction in convention size. No single interest is willing to absorb substantial reductions in numbers.

Many journalists and political scientists have called for fewer delegates, the figure most commonly mentioned being a total of 1,500 or less. The Republican party, of course, is well within that range, but the Democrats are not.

A simple way to cut back the number of Democratic delegates somewhat would be to eliminate fractional voting. There is considerable wisdom in the one-delegate-one-vote principle that the Republicans have long used. The exception made by the Democratic rules panel was in the smallest state delegations, where under the one-delegate-one-vote rule only a handful of people would have the opportunity to serve as delegates. Each state and the District of Columbia was guaranteed at least 20 delegates in order to accommodate candidate groupings, state and local factions, and demographic requirements.

On the whole, it is the objective of maximum participation for the party faithful that conflicts most with the objective of fewer delegates. The honor of being a convention delegate was long an

11. Republican National Committee, Delegates and Organizations Committee, Progress Report, Part II, *The Delegate Selection Procedures for the Republican Party* (1971), p. 8.

important patronage prize. Yet by no means are those from the old party machines the only ones to hold this view. Donald O. Peterson, chairman of the Wisconsin delegation to the 1968 Democratic convention, a supporter of Eugene McCarthy that year, and a member of the O'Hara Commission on Rules, spoke for many reformist Democrats in writing:

> From those who feel the Convention is too large, we have had proposals ranging from 500–1,500 people. But under present rules and considerations of time, even a Convention of this range could not achieve deliberation. Meaningful deliberation, however, *can* take place in the revised committees. Moreover, a smaller Convention would undoubtedly become a group of party elitists with little or no grass roots representation. A Convention that restricts representation will not serve our party well in the future.[12]

Advocates of smaller conventions question the extent to which one with 3,000 delegates is more representative than one with 1,000 delegates. In a nation of more than 200 million inhabitants, either represents a tiny fraction of the population, of the voters, and of party adherents. Apportionment rules and delegate selection procedures provide a much better test of a party's representativeness than does the number of participants. Moreover, it is questionable how much "meaningful deliberation" can take place in committees with 150 or 200 members or in state delegations that require a hotel ballroom or a theater for a caucus.

For the present, however, to make such a case is simply to cry in the wilderness. The extensive Democratic reforms after 1968 resulted in more delegates rather than fewer; and the Republicans seem predisposed to increase the size of their committees, though not yet that of their full assembly. If a more orderly and more democratic convention with real decision-making capability is to be built, politicians will not use fewer of their own kind to build it.

Prospects appear brighter for reducing the number of alternates. Since they do not usually have any official duty, the vast numbers

12. Letter from Donald Peterson to members of the O'Hara Commission on Rules, dated January 11, 1971.

of alternates are extraneous, and the post is essentially an honorary one. The alternate's job should not be abolished altogether, because there are times when a delegate dies or is incapacitated and a substitute is needed. Most proposals for fewer alternates suggest that each delegation be permitted a smaller number than its total of delegates. The O'Hara Commission at one time favored a ratio of one alternate for every three delegates but ultimately recommended that the Democratic National Committee decide. Ever since 1960, the Democrats have had fewer alternates than votes at each convention; that precedent will be followed in 1972. They could reduce the number further. A ratio of one alternate for every ten delegates does not seem unduly low in terms of actual need.

The Republicans, with far fewer delegates, have expressed almost no interest in moving from their one-vote-one-delegate-one-alternate pattern. Although their conventions have been more efficient, in this case they might do well to emulate the Democrats and consider reducing the ratio of alternates to delegates.

When politicians have turned their attention to reducing the number of people at conventions, most have recommended that fewer non-participants be permitted on the floor. While this approach is transparently self-serving, it *is* absurd that the participants have been crowded and even overwhelmed by other people at recent conventions.

Controlling access to the convention floor long has been viewed as a political and honorific task, and those holding it sometimes have tended not to take their duties very seriously. Accordingly, for the 1968 convention the Republicans abolished the positions of assistant doorkeeper and assistant sergeant-at-arms, which had been apportioned previously on the basis of one of each for every ten delegates. The Republicans now use professional security men exclusively, and party officials are satisfied that the new procedure makes for a more orderly convention.

The Democrats continued similar political jobs through the 1968 convention, although they used several professional security organizations as well. The inherent problem was compounded at the

1968 Democratic convention by a system of official admission cards for those with legitimate rights of access to the floor. If the card turned on a light when inserted in machines set up at entrances to the floor, the cardholder was admitted. This procedure received national publicity when the chairman of the insurgent New Hampshire delegation succeeded in activating the light with a Dartmouth College identification card. He told the story to television reporters, who had their own complaints about convention guards. Their reports about the incident cast discredit on the admission system and prompted the security men to march the delegate off for interrogation. The fiasco was complete when one of the guards charged that on the way to the interrogation, the delegate bit him. For 1972, the Democrats provided for a single security force, responsible to the committee on arrangements.

Forged tickets and floor passes have been a recurring problem. It frequently has been charged that the galleries were packed with illicit ticketholders who supported the presidential candidate favored by host-city leaders—Adlai Stevenson at Los Angeles in 1960, for example, and Abraham Lincoln at Chicago a century earlier. For 1972, the O'Hara Commission recommended that the convention arrangements committee determine how floor passes are to be distributed, give an equal number to each presidential candidate, and make public the number of passes and the identity of those holding them. Similar guidelines would apply to seats for visitors, with tickets apportioned fairly among the states according to delegation size. Care in producing and distributing tickets can prevent forgeries. The Republicans have worked out an intricate administrative system that effectively precludes duplicate tickets, and the Democrats could undoubtedly do the same.

In any discussion of the effects non-participants have on the convention, the central question is: Who shall be permitted on the floor? The delegates, certainly. Alternates, perhaps. Although some have favored keeping the alternates off the floor, they must be seated somewhere; they may need to cast a delegate's vote on short notice; and if they are off the floor, they will compete for space with honored guests, the press, and "the public"—generally supporters of one or another candidate. Convention and candidate staffs too need some passes—pages, messengers, guards, and political operatives. There is *some* controversy as to whether they should have access to the convention, but not a great deal. The real dispute is over the access of representatives of the news media.

A prominent official of the Democratic National Committee quipped ironically that he favored giving the news media all the space they asked for, because then he could stay home himself since there would be no room available for anyone else. Traditionally reporters have criticized politicians, especially the hapless Democrats, for their partisan excesses; and while journalists have attributed disorder at conventions to the number of delegates, alternates, and other politicians, they rarely have said much about the impact of members of their own profession. Yet it is widely acknowledged that the presence of reporters, and particularly that of television personnel and equipment, has a profound influence on the behavior of participants in the convention. Speakers address the television audience; delegates ask TV correspondents for autographs; the enormous central camera stand has been a visual obstacle for participants; and the television cameras and crews cause commotion wherever they go. Meanwhile, at each succeeding convention the press requests more floor passes and other perquisites for its coverage.

Many politicians understandably take a view of all this that is quite different from that of the news media. True, they cultivate the journalists and solicit their attention to the partisan deliberation. Yet, the politicians say, it is *their* convention; and if anyone is going to get fewer perquisites, it should be the press and not the party faithful. As Chapter 6 explains, the love-hate relationship between politicians and the news media has become more strained since the 1964 Republican and 1968 Democratic conventions and Vice President Spiro Agnew's criticisms of television news.

Yet many advocates of the open convention have sided with the news media in the debate. They view the media (particularly television) as a means of getting their story to the public if they fail to obtain recognition from the rostrum. Accordingly, when the O'Hara Commission considered the issue, supporters of the open convention voted consistently to admit representatives of all the media to the convention floor.

On grounds of fairness, each of the news media should be permitted to pursue its stories so long as it does not interfere with the work of the convention. To this end, reporters should be permitted limited access to the floor for short, fixed periods of time, as with the twenty-minute passes that have been used recently. They need this access to get their stories. The number of reporters on the floor at a given time, however, should be kept sufficiently small to prevent their disrupting the business of the convention. Even reporters would concede that the quality of press coverage bears little relationship to the number of journalists who have floor passes.

Television cameras and crews, after all, could be eliminated from the convention floor. The mobile cameras are not absolutely necessary. Zoom lenses and similar equipment allow television broadcasting of athletic contests; there is no reason why they cannot pick up equivalent detail for interviews, although they are less accurate in focusing on the details of action in crowds. Fixed cameras could be located at the sides or back of the hall and at other major sites off the floor. The necessary facilities could be arranged when the convention city and hall were selected. Removing the cameras would not necessitate removing television reporters or television pictures from the floor; it would simply eliminate a serious distraction from the political business at hand.

Procedural Rules and Deliberation

Decision-making at national conventions is profoundly influenced by its parliamentary rules. Occasionally, these rules may affect the outcome of a nomination; more typically, they affect the strategies of the participants. In either case, although the rules are a tedious subject to most laymen and many politicians, they constitute a political document delimiting the extent of fairness and democracy in convention deliberations.

Different politicians have different uses for the procedural rules. Candidates of course view them as a strategic or tactical device to help them win. Thus Dwight Eisenhower's managers in 1952 successfully proposed the "fair play" amendment to the rules that prevented many delegates who were contested from voting on their own credentials and paved the way for Eisenhower's nomination. (See Chapter 3.) Again, officers and officials charged with the management of the convention stress the judicious use of the rules as a means for promoting efficiency. By virtue of his position, the chairman—quintessentially, a Sam Rayburn—wants a clearly structured agenda, a minimum of debate, as few favorite son candidates as possible, and so on; all these simplify the job of chairman. In contrast, state delegations and individuals who identify with minority groups, dissidents, or insurgents seek rules that will promote broad representativeness and a convention that serves as an open forum for the expression of many viewpoints within the party. Hence they prefer rules that provide for extended debate, ease in obtaining roll call votes and polling of state delegations, and so on. Others, who are not necessarily allied with such groups, favor enough procedural flexibility to permit a fair and reasonable expression of their views. Finally, certain convention officials, members of candidate organizations, journalists, and others have as one of their concerns making conventions more interesting to the public. In many ways, they, and those who seek a hyper-efficient convention, work at cross-purposes, since a smoothly running conclave is often dull. But a convention at which insignificant speakers droned on until 4 o'clock in the morning would evoke equivalent yawns from most television viewers—if indeed they had not switched off their sets long before that time.

The two parties have different systems for adopting convention rules. Ordinarily each Republican convention considers the rules to be followed at the convention four years later. Recommendations for change have been debated and developed since the previous convention by panels of the national committee. This procedure has the advantage of letting all interested parties know well in advance what the ground rules will be for a particular convention. It effectively prevents rules from being made in the heat of a political battle for what is essentially momentary advantage, but it suffers from a certain inflexibility. If an unusual situation develops at the time of the convention, however, a proposal to change the rules can be considered through a motion to suspend the rules, or a change can be considered at the point when the rules for the convention are formally adopted. Traditionally the uncodified Democratic rules have been more flexible. Each Democratic convention has been governed by the rules of the previous convention until, in the process of permanent organization, it acts on the report of the committee on rules that will govern its own sessions. When rules have been a problem, the party typically has appointed a committee to study the issues and to recommend certain changes for the immediately following and subsequent conventions. The newly codified rules drawn up by the O'Hara Commission and approved by the Democratic National Committee will be used in 1972 and considered by that convention for permanent adoption. The Democratic procedure keeps the party open and sensitive to current issues—too sensitive for those who would prefer to keep the rules invulnerable to the pressures of the political moment.

In both parties the procedural rules have long been essentially those of the United States House of Representatives—which give members of the House who understand the rules a substantial advantage in intraparty decision-making. This pattern reflects the fundamentally congressional orientation of national convention officials. At the conventions since 1952, nine of the ten permanent chairmen have been members of Congress; seven were the party's ranking member in the House. Nine of the ten platform committee chairmen were members of Congress; four of the five Democrats were men on the leadership ladder of the House. While governors and other prominent partisans held other important posts, on the whole they were conspicuous by their absence from the two most influential convention offices. With experienced members of the House generally in charge of interpreting the rules of that body, those with no House experience who sought to outmaneuver the leadership were at a serious disadvantage.

The Republicans have sought to eliminate this disparity by changing to a more neutral set of rules. Their DO Committee has recommended that GOP conventions be governed by Robert's Rules of Order Revised, as the Republican National Committee now is under a rule adopted in 1968. Previously, the national committee, too, had operated under the House rules. Adopting Robert's Rules would serve the interests of insurgents, delegates attending their first convention, and rank-and-file delegates, none of whom is as familiar with the rules of the House as is the convention leadership. Newcomers are inherently at a disadvantage; they would be less so if parliamentary procedures were used with which they had had an opportunity to become familiar in their home states.

The Democrats have been more concerned with obtaining some written set of rules to cover the specific procedures of a convention. A prime example is the method of considering committee reports. Over the years, many Democrats have argued that to present to the assembled delegates a document as significant as the platform committee report only a few hours, or (as at the 1952 Democratic convention) minutes, before the final vote is unfair and undemocratic. On what basis could a delegate who was not a member of the platform committee rationally vote without access to the statement that was being voted upon? Presumably, it would be on the basis of cues from presidential candidates and the delegate's state representatives on the committee concerned. Thus committee reports have usually been approved quickly by conventions without any independent consideration by ordinary delegates.

To avoid this automatic acceptance by the delegates of reports they have not seen, strict procedures were needed that would permit real deliberation. The O'Hara Commission recommended that the state delegations select committee members for the Democratic convention. They would meet well in advance of the convention and distribute their reports (including any minority reports) several days before the convention opened—ninety-six hours before the convention in the case of the credentials committee, and ten days before for the platform and rules committees. In addition, thirty minutes would be allotted (unless more time were specifically provided by the rules committee) to the committee chairman to present its report; twenty minutes, with time divided equally between proponents and opponents, would be allowed for each amendment or minority report unless the convention specifically agreed to grant more. Voting on amendments and minority reports would come first and then the vote on the committee report. At the request of at least 10 percent of the committee members present and voting at a meeting, minority reports would be written and voted up or down on the convention floor. This would be a very strict rule for obtaining a minority report, particularly in situations where the party had an incumbent President. It would, however, provide for a vote on the merits of any minority report; procedural devices such as tabling the report or moving the previous question would specifically be prohibited. Altogether, these rules would provide a chance for all significant factions to make their case before the convention without unduly disrupting or prolonging the deliberative process.

On committee reports, the existing Republican rules are theoretically more flexible. They authorize the convention either to make its own rules about the presentation of reports or to abide by the practices of the House of Representatives. Actually, leaving the determination of procedure to the convention strengthens the hand of the leadership and lessens the chance for a dissident minority to make itself heard. The infrequence of Republican floor fights since 1952 suggests that the leaders have been able to confine conflict to the committee sessions. This is one instance where specifying procedures may give minority factions more influence than they have under open grants of authority to the delegates, who are usually responsive to the cues of the leaders on administrative matters.

More fundamentally, how do the rules help or hinder an ordinary delegate in an attempt to obtain the floor? "As long as they control the microphones," a young veteran insurgent remarked, "we can't get anywhere." The prospects for most delegates remain about as good as those for the sponsor of Joe Smith at the Republican convention in 1956. During the balloting for Vice President at that convention, a delegate from Nebraska sought to get to the podium and put a name in nomination other than Richard Nixon's. Since he cared little whose name it was and since he also sought to prevent the presiding officer from declaring that any prominent Republican he might mention had declined to be nominated, the delegate said that he wanted to nominate a "Joe Smith." He was not allowed to make the fictitious nomination.

Both parties require that a delegate be recognized by the chair in order to offer a motion. Ordinarily this is arranged before the session begins, for reasons of simple efficiency and because it is difficult for a presiding officer to see those on the floor who want recognition. The O'Hara Commission rules for the 1972 Democratic convention call for electronic communication between the floor and the convention chairman that will provide a means of making requests for recognition visible to the chairman, the delegates, and the news media. In general, both parties, and especially the presiding officers, take a dim view of the unknown delegate who without prior warning tries to make a speech or a motion. At a gathering the size of a national convention, the impulses of individuals must be channeled through their delegation leaders and members on the committees.

Recently both parties have streamlined the procedural rules for the convention's most important task—nominating candidates for President and Vice President. The reform panels in each party agreed in recommending that less attention be squandered on frivolous presidential candidates, that the time for nominating speeches be shortened, and that unspontaneous and rehearsed demonstrations for candidates be cut back. The Democrats' new rules for 1972 require each presidential candidate to present a petition indicating the support of at least 50 delegate votes in at least three states, with not more than 20 of the 50 being from a single state; no delegate is to be permitted to sign more than one candidate petition. The Republicans have no such rule at present, but the DO Committee has recommended requiring written proof of support in five states for a candidate to be considered a serious presidential contender. The Democrats' rules for 1972 will allow fifteen minutes' time for nominating and seconding speeches for presidential and vice presidential candidates. Under existing rules, the Republicans allot twenty-five minutes for presidential and twenty minutes for vice presidential nominating speeches. The DO Committee has recommended that the Republicans allow fourteen minutes for nominating and seconding speeches for major presidential and vice presidential candidates, with only five-minute speeches for favorite sons. The new Democratic rules formally prohibit demonstrations for candidates. The DO Committee has recommended limiting them to candidates who have substantial support. By enhancing the efficiency of convention deliberations, these rules will make the assemblies more coherent for both participants and observers, thereby permitting attention to be focused on the major issues and decisions of the gathering.

Proponents of fair convention procedure have been insistent on a more arcane aspect of nominations: the order of calling the roll of the states. They have pointed out that the traditional alphabetical order gave repeated and undue advantage to states that came at a strategic point on the list. Wisconsin and Wyoming, for example, were more often than most states in a position to put a candidate for a contested nomination over the top. New rules recommended by the O'Hara Commission and the DO Committee would change that. The Democratic rules for 1972 will determine the order of all the states by lot and use this list both for all roll calls and for seating arrangements in the hall. The new order for the roll calls is a matter of elementary fairness with which few would quarrel, although some Democratic traditionalists have complained that using the order for seating is unduly inflexible and eliminates the customary courtesies of choice seats for delegates from a President's home state, the host delegation, large contributors, and so on. The DO Committee plan for 1976 provides for determination by lot of the first state to be called in making nominations; the roll call would proceed alphabetically from that point. Roll calls other than those for nominations would continue to be on an alphabetical basis.

Many have sought to assure that no longer can the presidential nominee's choice of a running mate be forced on an unwilling convention. As one political veteran put it, "How can you entrust such a choice to a man with a hangover from the biggest celebration of his life?" In a century in which four presidents have died in office and two others have suffered serious illnesses on the job, the method of nominating the vice presidential candidate is of obvious concern. But no clearly superior method has yet been devised. There is no real way to prevent the preferences of the presidential nominees from becoming known if they want to divulge them. Of reforms that have been suggested, having the two run as a ticket at the convention would mean that runners-up in the presidential competition could not be considered for the vice presidential nomination. Selecting the vice presidential nominee first would limit the field to those who had no hope for the presidential nomination. Restricting the choice to the top three runners-up for the presidential nomination would circumscribe the convention and the presidential nominee in their attempts to select the strongest possible ticket.

Of the more grandiose proposals, electing the President and Vice President separately might mean that candidates from two different parties would be elected, which would surely create a difficult situation when it came to governing. Designating someone holding another high office as Vice President would involve the danger that the designee would be insufficiently informed to take over the presidency if necessary or would have to neglect the duties of the other office; in any case, the proposal does not settle the question of who should make the designation. Eliminating the office of vice president altogether would require a constitutional amendment and a reshuffling of the line of succession to the presidency but would not resolve the problem of how the second executive office would be filled.

Recent recommendations have been more modest. The Republicans, who have a Vice President in office, have been silent on the subject. The Democrats have sought to assure that candidates for Vice President other than the one preferred by the presidential nominee also have an opportunity to run at the convention and that the winner demonstrate substantial support among the delegates. In 1972, all Democratic candidates for Vice President will be required to submit petitions like those of the presidential candidates. This change will have little effect on the outcome of the deliberative process except that it will guard against the choice of a candidate who has little support and perhaps make the presidential nominee more sensitive to the wishes of the delegates in order to avoid the embarrassment of a substantial vote against the nominee's choice.

The major victory to date for proponents of fairness and democracy at conventions came at the 1968 Democratic conclave, when the winner-take-all unit rule was abolished. That was the most significant change that had been made in voting procedures since 1936, when the Democrats abandoned the two-thirds rule. The unit rule, never formally recognized by the GOP, gave each Democratic state using it maximum strength vis-à-vis other states; but since many delegations did not use it, the unit rule did not always enhance the position of the most populous or most strongly Democratic states. Its principal effect was to ensure that a delegation would be controlled by its majority faction and particularly its leader, who was often the governor. Thus it forced delegates who were in a minority faction within their state to cast their votes as the statewide majority wanted and not as they themselves preferred. Ending the unit rule would seem likely to work against rapid and efficient decision-making because it would permit a greater variety in points of view within each delegation. The change made in 1968, however, was less drastic than this because it merely freed delegates who were already at the convention. Further change in this direction can be expected at the 1972 Democratic convention, where the unit rule is prohibited at all stages of the delegate selection process.

Changes in voting procedure since 1968 have been less extensive. Both parties' reform panels considered electronic voting but abandoned the idea until there was more certainty about its implications—particularly regarding the honesty and reliability of the count. Ideally, electronic voting in which each delegate simply pushed the button of his or her choice would mean an open and efficient convention, albeit an undramatic one. Uncertain whether that ideal would work in practice, the DO Committee recommended that a Republican task force study the subject. Democratic advocates of an open convention concentrated on assuring that each delegate could make public his or her views on major issues. To the advantage of geographically dispersed minorities like the blacks and the disadvantage of geographically concentrated minorities like white southerners, the O'Hara Commission reinstated an old rule providing for a roll call vote on the demand of delegations from states with at least 20 percent of the delegates. (Previously a roll call vote was held on the demand of any eight delegations.) It also retained a rule requiring a poll of any delegation if any of its members requested one. Delegates were specifically authorized to ignore any state law or party regulation that required the unit rule. In sum, the delegates were freed to vote as they chose on the floor and to challenge any reported tally of their state. These procedures ran the risk of slowing down the proceedings. Presumably, threats of a roll call on voice votes or of polling a delegation on larger issues usually would be enough to keep the leadership fair. The Democrats evidently hoped that the likelihood of becoming persona non grata in the party would be enough to prevent a delegate from asking for unnecessary roll calls or polls. Ultimately, the workability of these rules depended upon the seriousness of purpose and good will of all those taking part in the convention, which was one reason that both the call and the convention rules required that all delegates be bona fide Democrats who would not support publicly any other ticket than that nominated by the convention.

Beyond the Rules

Whatever the size and procedures of the assembly, the capacity of a national convention to make decisions depends importantly on the delegates themselves. If the convention belongs to the delegates, they are charged not only with its authority but also with its responsibilities. The nature of the decision-making process rests on their consent and behavior, as well as on the formal rules.

At most conventions there is an inherent amount of disorder that can be kept within broadly manageable bounds. Whenever several thousand people are crowded into a hall, some confusion is inevitable. Moreover, the seats, aisles, and other facilities often have been inadequate to cope with the crush. The life style of the convention leads to what Herbert Agar has called "an atmosphere of frivolous indifference."[13] This is intensified by the simultaneous political excitement and lack of a sense of political efficacy on the part of many delegates. These problems could be diminished by reducing the size of the convention, its delegations, and its committees, which the parties have been unwilling to do; by increasing the physical comforts in the convention hall, which both Republicans and Democrats have attempted; and by amending procedural rules to give the delegates more of a sense of participation, which both the parties also have been trying to do.

But conventions must also be prepared to cope with a more extraordinary sort of disruption: the active expression of disapproval by sizable numbers of persons inside the convention hall. The Democrats who wore black armbands, linked arms, and sang

13. *The Pursuit of Happiness* (Houghton Mifflin, 1938), p. 134.

songs of protest in 1968 were delegates (and others) engaging in a partially organized protest. The motivations of the Republicans who screamed insults in 1964 are less clear.[14] Certainly, however, both groups consisted of people who found no more appropriate outlet for their displeasure.

To avoid a recurrence of massive alienation, the decision-making process must be fair and democratic; the delegates and also the public must believe that it is so. Without these conditions, the system will not always work. Unless the convention operates in an orderly fashion under procedures that are published, clear, and widely considered to be fair, adverse reactions by many participants are to be expected when feelings run high. Their reactions will be made known to the public through the news media; and if the situation is sufficiently dramatic, the public too may well react by repudiating the candidates and policies of the convention, and perhaps even the institution itself.

The rules can help. They can attack the problem at its source by providing arrangements that would keep those who are not loyal partisans from coming to the convention and that would permit the delegates who are selected to be recognized and to express their views fairly. They also can offer a means for coping with any disorders that nonetheless do occur.

Yet a major and inescapable defect of the convention system is its vulnerability to disruption. There are definite limits to the capacity of formal rules to deal with disruption that is caused by alienation. In a time of confrontation, it may be beyond the capacity of convention officials to get to the root of massive dis-

---

14. F. Clifton White and Theodore H. White each has emphasized that people seated in the galleries, and not delegates on the floor, were responsible for the shouting during the 1964 Republican platform debate. See F. Clifton White with William J. Gill, *Suite 3505: The Story of the Draft Goldwater Movement* (Arlington House, 1967), p. 398; and Theodore H. White, *The Making of the President 1964* (Atheneum, 1965), pp. 201–02. As the sociologist Gladys Lang has pointed out, disaffection also may be expressed by silence. That tradition was not followed in 1964 and 1968— perhaps because it was believed that silence would remain unnoticed in the torrent of convention noise, perhaps because the people involved preferred sound to silence in expressing themselves.

affection—particularly among delegates—and deal with it fairly, effectively, and swiftly. Extraordinary political and managerial skill is needed; and a large amount of luck does not hurt. Fundamentally, the convention simply reflects the principal divisions in the whole party; but it is extremely difficult to contain a faction bent on making further trouble in an already disorderly body of people.

Thus there are serious but necessary risks involved in fair and democratic rules. If a convention opens itself to dissident points of view, it must expect to hear them, and it may do well to anticipate disturbances. If it grants authority to the presiding officer to decide whether to turn on microphones in the state delegations or to throw the disorderly out of the hall, the convention can expect charges of repression and control by an elite. And if it encourages massive news coverage, it must be prepared to accept the risks to its image. This dilemma suggests both the profound significance and the inherent limitations of fairness and democracy in the rules of so subtle and complex an institution as the national convention.

Chapter Five

☆

WRITING THE PLATFORM

. . . such pledges are not written in snow.
Paul Tillett

IN CALLING FOR FAIRER and more democratic procedures, the new critics of conventions have not forgotten the writing of the party platform. Once again their recommendations have tended to clash with an ancient purpose of conventions: to create a party consensus on public issues.

The Significance of Platforms

The new emphasis on fairness and democracy in the writing of platforms differs markedly from the traditional view that they are meaningless. Thirty years ago, Wendell Willkie struck a familiar chord in referring to platforms as "fusions of ambiguity,"[1] signifying very little. Many observers have complained that, in George Wallace's words, there isn't a dime's worth of difference between the platforms of the two major parties. Others have contended that the platforms are meaningless in the sense that, once in office, the parties pay little attention to their promises, dismissing them as mere campaign oratory. Many of those who have criticized platforms as meaningless have been advocates of party government and have urged distinct programmatic platforms that would be binding on party candidates once they were elected.

Yet persuasive evidence exists that platforms are not meaning-

1. Quoted in Malcolm Moos and Stephen Hess, *Hats in the Ring: The Making of Presidential Candidates* (Random House, 1960), p. 102.

109

less. There is no doubt that party leaders long have taken platforms seriously. In recent years, there have been major disputes
over issues at the 1948 Democratic convention, the 1964 Republican convention, and the 1968 Democratic convention. Any of these
three would rank with the most explosive intraparty struggles of
U.S. history. Over all, leaders of party factions were sufficiently
in earnest about the stakes and issues of the platform to stage a
floor fight in four of the last ten conventions—those held from
1952 through 1968.

Recent research has verified that platforms are meaningful in
that they are significant over all, that the Republicans and Democrats have distinct programs, and that the programs are imple-
mented after a party wins the election. James L. Sundquist, secretary of the Democratic platform committee in 1960 (and 1968),
has pointed out that the platforms are simply one stage in the continuing process of party policymaking. In drafting their 1960 platform, Sundquist has written, the Democrats restated what had
been developed during the 1950s as party policy by the Democratic
Advisory Council, in previous platforms, in measures introduced
and statements made by Democrats in Congress, and in similar
party proposals.[2] Once in the White House, the Democrats tried
to implement these policies. The Republican process was much
the same: the platform was based on ideas and principles developed
within the party over time.

Other political scientists have undertaken statistical studies that
show the importance of platforms. In exhaustive analyses of the
content of major party platforms from 1944 through 1968, Gerald
Pomper was able to place each sentence of each platform in one of
three categories: simple rhetoric and fact, evaluation of the parties' records, and statements about future policies.[3] Table 5-1

2. James L. Sundquist, *Politics and Policy: The Eisenhower, Kennedy, and Johnson
Years* (Brookings Institution, 1968), pp. 389–415.

3. Gerald Pomper, *Elections in America: Control and Influence in Democratic Politics*
(Dodd, Mead, 1970), pp. 149–70; and "Controls and Influence in American Elections
(Even 1968)," *American Behavioral Scientist*, Vol. 13 (November–December 1969),
pp. 223–28.

TABLE 5-1. *Content of Democratic and Republican Party Platforms, 1952–68*

Percent

Party	1952	1956	1960	1964	1968	Mean, 1952–68
Democrats						
Rhetoric	18	14	20	20	21	19
Evaluations	31	42	26	64	25	38
Future policy	51	44	53	15	53	43
Republicans						
Rhetoric	9	15	21	11	13	14
Evaluations	46	47	22	44	22	36
Future policy	45	38	56	44	65	50

Sources: Adapted from Gerald Pomper, *Elections in America: Control and Influence in Democratic Politics* (Dodd, Mead, 1970), p. 159; and "Controls and Influence in American Elections (Even 1968)," *American Behavioral Scientist*, Vol. 13 (November–December 1969), p. 224.

Note: Details may not add to 100 percent due to rounding.

shows the results of his categorizations for the period covered by this book. Pomper found that although the percentages varied from year to year, on the whole less than a quarter of the platform statements consisted of mere bombast or rhetoric. On an average, just over one-third of the platform declarations were evaluations of the party records—pointing with pride by the Ins and viewing with alarm by the Outs, to be sure, but also calling attention to a serious standard for making voting decisions. The remainder of the platform statements, Pomper found, were pledges dealing with future public policy. These pledges typically accounted for nearly half the platform statements.

Pomper also categorized the pledges according to their specificity and found that slightly over 60 percent clustered near the more specific end of his spectrum—pledges to maintain an existing policy (such as continued federal support for medical research), expressions of goals and concerns (encouraging resettlement of Arab refugees where room and opportunity exist), pledges of action (tax incentives to encourage modernization of corporate plant and equipment), and detailed pledges (repeal of section 14[b] of the

Taft-Hartley Act).[4] Pomper's analysis thus showed that platforms have been meaningful statements of partisan views and intentions.

Pomper also sought to determine whether there have been significant differences between the parties' platforms; he answered that question in the affirmative. The parties, he found, were distinctive, not primarily in specific disagreement but in differing emphases. He discovered that over half the 2,245 pledges in the platforms from 1944 to 1964 were made by only one party; about one-third were made by both parties; and on the remainder of the pledges the parties were in direct conflict. This pattern resulted, Pomper concluded, because the two parties appealed to different constituencies. The Republicans consistently made more pledges about defense and government, and the Democrats paid more attention to labor and welfare. Any direct conflict that existed between the parties was proportionately highest on bread-and-butter economic issues, where competing interest groups sought tangible benefits. Bipartisan agreement was greatest on foreign policy and civil rights issues—although when Pomper subsequently looked at the 1968 platforms, he found that the Republicans in pursuing a southern strategy had retreated to what was essentially rhetoric on civil rights, while the Democrats continued to make specific pledges.[5]

In considering how well the parties have performed in fulfilling their pledges, Pomper concluded that they have done much better than is generally realized. Of the 2,245 pledges he counted in major party platforms from 1944 through 1964, 1,399 were sufficiently precise that the extent of their implementation could be tested. Of

4. Pomper, *Elections in America*, pp. 157–58.

5. *Ibid.*, pp. 168–75, 193–95; Pomper, "Controls and Influence in American Elections (Even 1968)," p. 227. Recently J. Zvi Namenwirth and Harold D. Lasswell have concluded, on the basis of a computerized content analysis of selected nineteenth and twentieth century major party platforms, that the documents during the recent period have become more similar and more programmatic. This, they contend, is because the party leaders are now more knowledgeable about, and responsive to, the attitudes of the public and have consciously moved to accommodate them. "The Changing Language of American Values: A Computer Study of Selected Party Platforms," Vol. 1, Comparative Politics Series (Sage, 1970).

this group, 72 percent had been fulfilled through 1966. Table 5-2, constructed from Pomper's data, shows the breakdowns by party categories. As one might expect, bipartisan pledges had the best record of success; 85 percent of them were adopted. The party in power, however, did nearly as well, with 79 percent of its pledges fulfilled; and even the party that lost the election was able to redeem over half its pledges. Moreover, the rate of fulfillment for in-party and bipartisan pledges has accelerated markedly in recent years. These data support the contention that political leaders take platform pledges seriously after the campaign is over. The platforms provide the agenda for executive officials planning the President's program and for legislators who consider it and develop additional proposals. The platforms, as Paul T. David has pointed out, have effectively become national plans.[6]

TABLE 5-2. *The Fulfillment of Testable Major Party Platform Pledges, 1944–66*
Percent

Type of pledge	Pledges fulfilled	Pledges defeated	Pledges on which no action was taken	Number testable as a percentage of total pledges
Bipartisan	85	13	2	33
In-party	79	16	5	31
Out-party	53	27	20	36

Source: Adapted from Gerald Pomper, *Elections in America: Control and Influence in Democratic Politics* (Dodd, Mead, 1970), p. 186.

Proponents of responsible party government, who began writing many years before Pomper's studies were made, have favored platforms that are not only programmatic, but also binding. Ideally, they say, a party would consist of people who are united by common beliefs and purposes; political leaders would be selected after they had stated their beliefs and pledged to follow certain specific policies if they were elected. Knowing this, the voters would choose between or among the candidates primarily on the bases of

6. Paul T. David, "Party Platforms As National Plans," *Public Administration Review*, Vol. 31 (May–June 1971), pp. 303–15.

the party's platform and subsequent campaign statements, which would differ sharply from those of the opposition. The elected leaders would work to fulfill their party's promises. Disloyalty would be grounds for explusion from the party.

Such parties do not and will not exist in the United States, if indeed they do anywhere. The major parties, reflecting the nation, are heterogeneous in social composition and in political philosophy. Realizing this, party leaders have been reluctant to purge their dissidents. As Pomper has shown, there is significant policy content in the struggle between the parties, but not the stark contrast that proponents of responsible party government would prefer. Sharpening the alternatives further would tend to break up their coalitions and splinter the parties; dissidents would start their own factions, which might result in new parties. The behavior of unreconstructed southerners since the Democratic civil-rights plank was adopted in 1948 shows how they might proceed. The system envisioned by proponents of responsible party government simply could not work within the U.S. setting of federalism and the formal separation of powers in the national government. Given such major constraints, binding programmatic platforms represent a utopian dream.

Tacitly recognizing all this, politicians have spent little time contemplating the responsible party government theory in recent discussion. Instead, when deliberating about the future of the platform, they have concerned themselves with the more important issue of how control over writing the platform has been, and should be, distributed.

Drafting the Platforms

An elaborate process for drafting a written version of national party policy has developed since the 1840 Democratic convention "adopted a statement of party principles called a 'platform,'"[7]

7. Paul T. David, Ralph M. Goldman, and Richard C. Bain, *The Politics of National Party Conventions* (Brookings Institution, 1960), p. 19.

perhaps the first such statement with that name. In both parties, drafting has been the responsibility of a committee on resolutions, consisting typically of a male and a female delegate from each state and territory, selected by their respective delegations. The platform committee chairman has been named by the national committee several months before the convention and approved formally by the delegates at their opening session. The platform committees have met several days in advance of the convention—usually during the previous week—to hear testimony from party leaders and interest group spokesmen. Thereafter they have gone into executive session to consider draft platform statements. The platform approved by the committee has been presented to the full convention. During the years with which this study is concerned, from 1952 through 1968, the convention has never rejected a platform committee report—or even amended it significantly.

Although the writing of party platforms has involved extensive canvassing of popular views, no one who has studied the process has concluded that popular influence on the platforms has been more than minimal and indirect. To be sure, public opinion established the wide boundaries within which the platform-writers worked; but the drafting of platforms, like the drafting of legislation by congressional committees, has been done by political leaders—presidents or presidential candidates, the platform committee chairmen and members, and their staffs. Platform writers have been free to negotiate among political leaders—far more than have congressmen who are close to a particular constituency back home.

There is virtual unanimity among politicians and among writers on politics that the platform committee hearings have been, in Walter Bagehot's terms, more formal than efficient. The committee members have *not* congregated, listened attentively to the witnesses' statements, and then met like a jury to decide among them. The hearings may be more accurately described as a televised forum for party and interest group leaders to express views that are already familiar to members of the committee. Witnesses have provided themes and information, and they have enjoyed national stature in giving their testimony; but they rarely have changed the minds of committee members. The latter have attended the public proceedings irregularly. A few have never come at all. Those who have participated have taken the most interest in executive sessions, where except on a few controversial issues their options were limited to drafts prepared for them by the staff and the drafting committee appointed by the chairman.

Only a small fraction of platform issues have been controversial. On most matters of public policy each party agrees internally, often much more than the general public realizes. As Gerald Pomper noted, more than half the platform has consisted of rhetoric and evaluations of the two parties' records. Such statements are unlikely to evoke much debate at a partisan meeting. Moreover, many of the remaining statements—pledges of future party action—have been either firmly established party policies with a broad consensus of support or specific matters of interest to only a few groups and individuals. The residual issues of great national consequence and deep intraparty division—civil rights, Vietnam, or political extremism—have been the subjects of extended platform debates.

THE STRATEGIC ENVIRONMENT

The character of the platform has depended to a great extent on the presidential politics of the day: whether the party was In or Out and whether the President was standing for reelection. When a party has been in control of the White House and the President has sought to stay there four more years, the platform-writing process has been dominated by his wishes. During the period studied here, this has been the case twice: for the Republicans in 1956 and for the Democrats in 1964.

Several months before the 1956 Republican convention opened, the national committee solicited and collected proposals for the platform. Top administration officials prepared statements and cleared them with the White House staff. Connecticut Senator

Prescott S. Bush, an Eisenhower Republican who was named chairman of the platform committee, discussed its worth with the President, former President Herbert Hoover, and Secretary of State John Foster Dulles. The committee held an organizing session on August 15, promptly opened hearings, and went into executive session to begin drafting on August 17. Only over civil rights was there any threat of disagreement, which White House assistant Sherman Adams quietly dispelled. As "White House aides superintended the drafting under tight security conditions,"[8] the planks were written and approved. Presented by members of the Cabinet, the platform committee report was quickly adopted by the convention.

The making of the 1964 Democratic platform was even more streamlined. With President Johnson a candidate for election in November, the convention was what he chose to make it. The week before the convention opened, the platform committee held hearings in Washington and in Atlantic City, the convention site. Seeking broad support, the Democrats adopted several proposals made by moderate Republicans—notably a condemnation of extremist political groups—that had been rejected a month earlier by the GOP convention. There was little overt controversy as the committee approved a draft document entitled "One Nation, One People." With equal alacrity, no dissent, and probable boredom, the convention approved it by voice vote on the second day of its meeting—far sooner than is customary.

When the President in office has not sought another term, he has shared authority over the platform with the leading presidential candidates in his party (or their lieutenants), the platform committee chairman, and the members of the committee. This was essentially the case for Presidents Truman in 1952, Eisenhower in 1960, and Johnson in 1968, although the Johnson influence on the Vietnam plank was somewhat greater because of the remote, but to some politicians real, possibility that he might decide to run

8. Charles A. H. Thomson and Frances M. Shattuck, *The 1956 Presidential Campaign* (Brookings Institution, 1960), p. 178.

again if the platform criticized his Vietnam policy or if he were otherwise displeased.

The typical situation with a lame-duck president existed when the 1952 Democratic platform was written. The Democratic National Committee appointed a 21-member executive committee, chaired by House Majority Leader John W. McCormack of Massachusetts, to serve as a preliminary platform committee. This panel began public hearings the week before the convention opened. After five days of hearings, McCormack appointed a 19-member drafting committee, "heavily weighted with representatives from the Congressional wing of the party."[9] Meanwhile, the White House staff had prepared a series of draft planks at the President's request. Believing that the committee should write its own platform, Chairman McCormack, in conjunction with his advisers, proceeded to revise the White House proposals substantially. A White House staff team reworked the McCormack draft with him; the resulting draft went to the committee. Controversy over civil rights was eventually avoided by skillful wording. Once the revisions had passed the committee, the full convention approved the platform report by voice vote, although the Georgia and Mississippi delegations asked to be recorded as voting "nay" because of the civil rights section.

The 1968 Democratic platform, responsible for more drama than the presidential nomination, shows the maximum influence of a retiring President on the process. Determined that his party should give his administration a vote of confidence on Vietnam, Lyndon Johnson through his supporters worked his will on the Vietnam plank almost as a President who was running in November would have. Witnesses were an initial issue; a peace plank supporter threatened to hold separate hearings if opponents of the administration's Vietnam policy were not added to the original list. Statements on Vietnam were written and rewritten. In the words of reporters who were on the scene, "draft peace planks

9. Edward F. Cooke, "Drafting the 1952 Platforms," *Western Political Quarterly*, Vol. 9 (September 1956), p. 704.

were fluttering around like confetti."[10] Party leaders struggled to write a statement that would be acceptable to President Johnson *and* Vice President Humphrey *and* the peace forces. In the end, it could not be done. Johnson not only refused to budge but also, through intermediaries, defied his critics; Humphrey considered himself politically and morally bound to Johnson; and the supporters of the peace plank were unmoved. The Johnson position prevailed in committee by a 62–35 vote. There ensued a four-hour floor debate at the obscure time of Wednesday afternoon. It resulted in a vote of 1,567¾ to 1,041¼ against the minority peace plank. The committee report then was approved by voice vote, but few rejoiced.

The situation at the Republican convention in 1960 was the reverse of that of the Democrats in 1968; the Republican platform, although it was written when the GOP had a President in the White House and an heir apparent who was expected to succeed him, was very much the product of bargaining among party groups. The situation was almost like that of a party out of power.

Fissures within the party, kept latent four years earlier by adherence to presidential wishes, became manifest as the party leadership changed. Platform committee chairman Charles H. Percy, then president of the Bell & Howell Company, provided his committee with a draft platform written at the White House and tentatively cleared with the President, the Vice President, and other party leaders.[11] On their opening day, the platform committee assembled to hear addresses by leading Republicans and then

10. Lewis Chester, Godfrey Hodgson, and Bruce Page, *An American Melodrama: The Presidential Campaign of 1968* (Dell, 1969), p. 594.

11. Paul Tillett, "The National Conventions," in Paul T. David (ed.), *The Presidential Election and Transition 1960–61* (Brookings Institution, 1961), p. 37; John H. Kessel, "Political Leadership: The Nixon Version," in Paul Tillett (ed.), *Inside Politics* (Oceana, 1962), p. 43. Accounts of the celebrated 1960 Republican platform negotiations may also be found in Karl A. Lamb, "Civil Rights and the Republican Platform: Nixon Achieves Control," in Tillett (ed.), *Inside Politics*, pp. 59–84; Daniel M. Ogden, Jr., and Arthur L. Peterson, *Electing the President: 1964* (Chandler, 1964), pp. 54–61; Richard M. Nixon, *Six Crises* (2nd ed., Doubleday, 1969), pp. 313–16; and Theodore H. White, *The Making of the President 1960* (Pocket Books, 1961), pp. 229–47.

regrouped into eight subcommittees for deliberation. Four days after the committee had assembled, their drafts were completed. It quickly became known that Governor Nelson A. Rockefeller of New York, who had once been a candidate for the nomination and was no team player, wanted stronger civil rights and defense sections. Threatened with a floor fight over the platform and the prospect of Rockefeller's sitting out the campaign—either or both of which might mean losing New York State and possibly the election in November—Vice President Nixon sought out Rockefeller in the latter's Manhattan apartment. Nixon has written that the "most sticky area"[12] of discussion was national defense, presumably because Nixon flatly refused to criticize the administration's policy as Rockefeller had been doing.

Once the agreement had been made, the platform committee had to be persuaded to adopt it—which was no easy task. Like their Democratic predecessors in 1952, the members were convinced of their own importance, believing that only they had the authority to write the platform. Moreover, President Eisenhower was incensed that Rockefeller had persuaded Nixon to endorse statements that were even mildly critical of his administration; GOP professionals supported their President. Arizona Senator Barry M. Goldwater, leading spokesman of the conservative faction, called the Nixon-Rockefeller pact the "Munich of the Republican party."[13] Nixon and his staff had to work out new planks that were acceptable to Eisenhower, Rockefeller, the committee, and themselves.

Nixon made the bargain stick. John H. Kessel, a political scientist who was at the scene, has reported that while one group of Nixon and Rockefeller staff members worked out the new wording, another team systematically rounded up delegate support. When the civil rights subcommittee refused to accept the Nixon-Rockefeller proposals, Nixon held a press conference at which he pointedly endorsed them. He then met personally with recalcitrant

12. Nixon, *Six Crises*, p. 315.
13. Quoted in White, *The Making of the President 1960*, p. 239.

delegates, telling them that the civil rights proposals represented Nixon's own views, although he was not committed to the specific language, and threatening that if the committee refused to accept the proposals, he would fight them on the floor.[14] Karl Lamb, another political scientist who observed the proceedings at first hand, has described in detail the negotiations within the platform committee. In addition to Nixon's own efforts, Lamb stresses those of Charles Percy; of Representative Melvin R. Laird of Wisconsin, the vice chairman and a skilled parliamentarian who assumed the gavel when the showdown votes came; and of such advocates of party unity as former national chairman Leonard Hall, a Nixon leader.[15] Six key votes occurred in the full committee; while the southern-conservative faction and the Nixon-Rockefeller forces each won three, the latter clearly triumphed. Given those results and the trauma that had preceded them, neither side took the issue to the convention floor.

In the party out of power, there has been even less centralized control over the preparation of the platform; it has been the subject of bargaining among many groups and individuals—the presidential candidates, the chairman, the committee, the staff, and supporters of various viewpoints. In 1952, 1964, and 1968, the Republican platform was a battleground of candidate groups as well as others; in 1956 and 1960, the Democratic platform was debated less by the candidate organizations than by those who were interested primarily in the civil rights issue.

The Republican experience in 1968 is typical. After the party schisms of 1964, national chairman Ray C. Bliss had created a partywide Republican Coordinating Committee that met from 1965 to 1968 to study selected issues; its reports were issued periodically and published in a single volume just before the opening of the national convention.[16] The Republicans in 1968 also had the

---

14. Kessel, "Political Leadership," pp. 46–48.
15. Lamb, "Civil Rights and the Republican Platform," pp. 68–84.
16. Republican Coordinating Committee, *Choice for America: Republican Answers to the Challenge of Now* (Republican National Committee, July 1968).

benefit of a volume of papers on domestic issues, compiled under the editorship of Melvin Laird,[17] who had been chairman of the 1964 platform committee.

When the public platform hearings began, many statements by leading Republicans that were presented at morning hearings of the full committee incorporated Republican Coordinating Committee task force reports. At the afternoon sessions, seven platform subcommittees heard witnesses for various interest groups. On the fourth day the committee went into executive session to draft its report. A 7,000-word draft was submitted as a working document by the chairman, Senate Minority Leader Everett M. Dirksen of Illinois.

Hard bargaining like that of 1960 followed. While there was no formal compact between Nixon and Rockefeller, their supporters once again combined to work out a compromise that was acceptable to both. Essentially, it included views that were liberal by Republican standards and, as in 1960, thereby avoided a floor fight on the platform like that of 1964. As in the Democratic party, the principal controversy concerned Vietnam. A draft approved by the foreign policy and national security subcommittee criticized the Democratic administration for insufficient aggressiveness and a failure to delegate adequate authority to the military. Supporters of California Governor Ronald Reagan favored this general position; the Nixon and Rockefeller groups did not. The successful compromise plank, which used language suggested by both the Nixon and the Rockefeller forces, as well as by others, stressed giving the South Vietnamese primary responsibility for defending themselves[18]—which subsequently became the Vietnamization policy of the Nixon administration. There was no minority report; the platform committee recommendations were approved on the floor by voice vote.

17. Melvin R. Laird (ed.), *Republican Papers* (Doubleday, 1968).
18. Theodore H. White, *The Making of the President 1968* (Atheneum, 1969), pp. 245–46; Congressional Quarterly Service, *The Presidential Nominating Conventions, 1968* (Congressional Quarterly, 1968)

ROLE OF THE CANDIDATES

While incumbent presidents standing for election have dominated their conventions and obtained platforms that pledge to continue the policies of their administrations, other presidential candidates have not been in such a commanding position. Not all of them have been able to exercise much leadership on the platform, nor have they even been interested in doing so. Eugene McCarthy, who entered a presidential campaign primarily to start a dialogue there on a major issue, and Nelson Rockefeller, who stubbornly pursued platform victories when his own candidacy was dead, both have been exceptions to the general rule that presidential candidates understandably are preoccupied with winning the nomination.

When candidates have turned their attention to platform matters, they have given leading supporters or staff subordinates the task of looking after their interests as the platform is written. For example, Connecticut Representative (and former Governor) Chester Bowles, who was serving officially as John Kennedy's principal foreign affairs adviser at the time when Bowles was named as chairman of the 1960 Democratic platform committee, has written that Kennedy gave a draft platform "only a cursory glance,"[19] when Bowles showed it to him in May 1960. Bowles adds that Robert Kennedy, his brother's campaign manager, read another draft more thoroughly the day before it was presented and offered no suggestions; Bowles doubts that the elder brother read it seriously until after he was nominated.[20] Others in the Kennedy circle were involved directly in writing the civil rights section of the statement.

The Kennedy pattern was followed by the winning Democratic aspirants of other years. Ever the reluctant candidate, Adlai Stevenson took no leading role in writing the 1952 and 1956 plat-

19. Chester Bowles, *Promises to Keep: My Years in Public Life, 1941–1969* (Harper & Row, 1971), p. 291.
20. *Ibid.*

forms. Yet he began his 1952 acceptance speech with the words, "I accept your nomination—and your program."[21] In 1956 two other Democrats with presidential ambitions, New York Governor Averell Harriman and Tennessee Senator Estes Kefauver, led an unsuccessful fight to strengthen the civil rights section of the platform; Stevenson stayed out of the battle. In 1968, backers of Hubert Humphrey proposed a statement on Vietnam known to have his tacit support; it lost in committee to the one preferred by President Johnson.

The Republican tradition is very different; in the years studied, presidential candidates and their supporters nearly always have been central figures in the platform-writing process. In 1952 Eisenhower supporters concentrated on credentials and rules disputes rather than on the platform; winning the first two controversies was essential to victory in the presidential contest, and the platform was not. Consequently, as Austin Ranney has observed, "Taft got the platform and Eisenhower got the nomination."[22] In 1960 and 1968, however, Richard Nixon intervened to get the platform he wanted and to solidify his support in the Rockefeller wing of the party. Barry Goldwater in 1964 was less active in shaping the document than his supporters were, but it certainly reflected their common views.[23]

ROLE OF THE CHAIRMAN

The chief official of the committee has been in a position to exercise decisive influence on the platform and sometimes has done so. During the years 1952 through 1968 most platform committee chairmen were congressional leaders. The Democratic chairman was usually the second-ranking House Democrat, with the top-ranking House Democrat serving as permanent chairman of the

21. Adlai E. Stevenson, *Major Campaign Speeches of Adlai E. Stevenson 1952* (Random House, 1953), p. 7.

22. "The Platforms, the Parties, and the Voters," *Yale Review*, Vol. 42 (Autumn 1952), p. 17.

23. On the 1964 Republican platform, see John H. Kessel, *The Goldwater Coalition: Republican Strategies in 1964* (Bobbs-Merrill, 1968), pp. 106–15.

convention. Exceptions to this pattern came in 1960, when national chairman Paul M. Butler by-passed the congressional elders and selected Chester Bowles for the platform committee assignment; and in 1968, when House Democratic Whip Hale Boggs of Louisiana moved up, while Majority Leader Carl Albert of Oklahoma served as permanent chairman in place of the elderly Speaker John McCormack. The Republicans, too, often turned to Congress for platform committee chairmen; to Senator Eugene Millikin of Colorado in 1952, Senator Prescott Bush of Connecticut in 1956, Congressman Melvin Laird of Wisconsin in 1964, and Senate Minority Leader Everett Dirksen of Illinois in 1968. The exception was Charles Percy, a future senator who in 1960 was a president of a corporation and a protégé of President Eisenhower.

The extent to which these chairmen exercised real influence varied with political circumstances. Those who served when their party was led by a President who sought another term (Bush and Albert) carried out his wishes. Those who were chairmen when the presidential candidates or their organizations became significantly involved in platform negotiations could not ignore their views. Depending on the situation at the presidential level of the party, the platform committee chairmen did have considerable opportunity to exercise leadership: appointing subcommittee and drafting committee members, selecting a staff, arranging for witnesses, overseeing the drafting, and negotiating among interests. While measuring and comparing influence in past situations is never satisfactorily scientific, clearly one strong chairman was Melvin Laird in 1964. The circumstances were propitious; Goldwater, certain to be the nominee, engaged in no platform negotiations outside Laird's domain. But Laird himself chose to lead and was able to do so. In a profoundly divided convention, he dominated the platform panel; only three of its members voted against the draft in committee. On the other hand, Charles Percy—although an able chairman in many ways—was unable to contain single-handedly the intraparty struggle over the 1960 platform. Richard Nixon himself had to persuade the most stubbon delegates.

ROLE OF COMMITTEE MEMBERS

There was great variety in the experience, knowledge, and interest of platform committee members during the 1952–68 period. As was noted earlier, the committee members—like members of Congress—were more attentive during the executive sessions when platform drafts were actually being considered than they were during the reading of testimony by witnesses. Some were sufficiently concerned to discuss the issues presented in testimony; others remained silent or failed to go to hearings at all.

Only once did committee members stage a successful revolt: in 1960 the Democratic platform panel strengthened the Bowles-Kennedy civil rights statement. Also the 1960 Republican platform committee balked when members felt that their functions were being usurped by the Nixon-Rockefeller pact. Less well remembered is the resentment on the part of the 1952 Democratic committee of White House efforts to write a platform when President Truman was not running for renomination. In addition, in each of the years other than those when an incumbent President was seeking another term, there was significant conflict within the committee, which was resolved either at that level (for both parties in 1952 and the Republicans in 1960 and 1968) or on the floor (the Republicans in 1964 and the Democrats in 1956, 1960, and 1968). Clearly then, an important segment of the committee members have been active in the deliberations and drafting.

One notable pattern of platform committee operations has been the significant structural difference between the parties and over time. The Republicans have tended to specialize, dividing into subcommittees for hearings and executive sessions. The Democrats have made more use of their full committee for both formal and working sessions, although drafting is carried out in a subcommittee. Furthermore, the two parties have tended to move toward more similar structural patterns, with the Republicans inaugurating full committee sessions in 1960 and using them more extensively in 1968, and the Democrats in the latter year dividing into catchall hearing panels for the consideration of all issues except Vietnam.

The structure of the platform committee has affected the patterns of influence. Karl Lamb has noted that Republican subcommittee members in 1960 were appointed largely on the basis of their own preferences; all got their first or second choice. He adds: "Almost without exception, the southern members [of the platform committee] asked to serve on the subcommittee on civil rights and immigration. . . ."[24] Although only five of the thirteen members selected for that subcommittee were southerners, they were a much more influential faction, particularly in combination with northern conservative allies on the subcommittee, than was the southern bloc on the full platform committee. The views of their faction, moreover, were far removed from those of the pro–civil rights subcommittee chairman, New York State Assembly Speaker Joseph F. Carlino. As Lamb points out, making the subcommittees the working units of the platform panel and appointing the members primarily on the basis of self-selection meant that the members served on the unit in which they had the most intense interest and deepest convictions.[25] There was a similar pattern in the 1968 Republican platform subcommittee on foreign policy and national security, which produced a hawkish statement on Vietnam that was changed substantially in the full committee. Over all, subcommittees that deviated sharply from the full committee because of differences in constituency tended to be overruled in the larger panel.

A full platform committee or nonspecialized subcommittees, in contrast, were more likely to contain a wide spectrum of views on any subject considered. Accordingly, they were less likely to be controlled by an unrepresentative bloc with intense interests. Nor could a full committee selected by the respective state delegations be stacked by the committee chairman, as subcommittees could be. A full committee or a nonspecialized subcommittee, however,

24. Lamb, "Civil Rights and the Republican Platform," p. 60.
25. *Ibid.*, p. 61.

could be unrepresentative of the whole convention because the committees and subcommittees were apportioned differently. The less populous states, for example, were relatively stronger in the platform committees, which were apportioned on the basis of two delegates for each state, than they were in the convention as a whole, where most votes were based on state population or party voting records (see Chapter 2). While this difference in constituencies would lead one to expect that the convention at least occasionally would overturn the platform committee report, this has not happened. The principal reason is probably that the threat of a floor fight that might overturn the decision of the committee (as occurred in the Democratic party in 1948) has been enough to persuade its members not to take stands that the full convention might not support.

ROLE OF THE STAFF

The contributions of staff members to the platform have been less visible, but they are very important in each party. Recruited mostly from Capitol Hill, from national party committees, and from the academic world, the staffs of the platform committees and of the presidential candidates concerned with the platform have acted as the compilers of recommendations, formulators of language, and occasionally negotiators among factions. Although less well known to most citizens, the staff members are as much national political figures as are their more famous political mentors.

The policy recommendations compiled by the staffs have varied in nature, depending on whether their party was in or out of power. When it was In, the principal sources of proposals were presidential statements and information obtained from the various federal agencies and departments. When the party was Out, candidate statements, previous platforms, and congressional and national committee sources assumed greater importance. During the period covered here, the party out of power produced increasingly elaborate reports and recommendations, almost like those of a shadow government. Such was the work of the Democratic Advisory

Council between 1957 and 1960, the Republican Critical Issues Council and Coordinating Committee after the 1960 and 1964 elections, and the Democratic Policy Council established following the 1968 election. The work of Democrats and Republicans in Congress produced additional material that was used by platform committees and candidate staffs.

The role of the staffs in drafting platform language and promoting political bargains is more difficult to trace but is of obvious significance. Anyone who suggests wording has an opportunity to influence policy. Staff members of the platform committee, the candidates, other party leaders, and, in the case of the party in power, the White House and the executive branch performed this function for both Republicans and Democrats. Staff members also take part in political negotiations, but their efforts are obscured by the necessarily low visibility of such operations.

Aware of the potential influence of their staffs, prudent politicians have selected them carefully in order to maintain control over subsequent developments. For example, Melvin Laird as chairman of the 1964 Republican platform committee entrusted drafting to a committee on style and language that included two former Eisenhower assistants and a Goldwater man—an ideological balance that represents one method of controlling a staff group. (As time passed, one of the three-man group became involved with the Goldwater campaign and another with Scranton's; hence the third of the trio did most of the drafting.) Again, in 1960, with the active support of national chairman Paul Butler, a different strategy was chosen by the Democratic platform chairman, Chester Bowles. He selected a liberal staff that would presumably ensure the liberal platform that he and Butler wanted.

ROLE OF ORDINARY DELEGATES

The preceding analysis concludes that the platform-writing process has been dominated by top party leaders: by the President when the party is in power and the incumbent seeks to run again; by the candidates, the retiring President, and the platform committee chairman and members when the party is in power but the President will not run again; and by the candidates and the platform committee chairman and members when the party is out of power. Nonetheless, significant policy debates have taken place at the convention whenever major issues were being debated at the mass level of the party. The Republicans have typically resolved such conflicts within the platform committee, the only exception being the bitter 1964 fight. The Democrats more often have taken divisive issues to the convention floor. In both parties the platform committee report has always prevailed. Formal debates before the full convention have consisted of statements made by speakers selected by leaders of the two sides. And for obvious reasons most of these speakers have been prominent and persuasive party leaders rather than passionate but unknown delegates. Most ordinary delegates have participated directly only in the ultimate decision for or against the committee report.

Alternatives

Because of the character of past platform deliberations, critics have sought structural reforms, most of them aimed at facilitating increased opportunity for participation by ordinary delegates and forging a closer link between the views of the voters and those of the presidential candidate and his party. Defenders of the existing system have argued that if more ideological or "amateur" delegates took part in writing the platform, it might be less moderate; and that a less moderate platform would inhibit party unity— particularly if the candidate wanted to rewrite it, as Richard Nixon did in 1960 and 1968.

The Democrats' O'Hara Commission on Rules considered various options and voted for a series of changes. (The Republicans' DO Committee lacked the authority to consider reform of the platform-writing process.) Among the O'Hara Commission's recommendations were the following:

• All committees, including the platform panel, would consist of up to 150 members allocated approximately in proportion to the size of each state delegation.

• The chairman, a fifteen-member drafting committee, and its chairman would be elected by the full committee members at their first meeting.

• As in 1960, regional platform hearings would be held around the country.

• Any individual would be authorized to submit written material or oral testimony to the platform committee.

• Before the first platform committee meeting, the Democratic national chairman would provide each member with a draft document listing leading issues and alternatives.

• A representative of each presidential candidate would be permitted to serve as a non-voting member of the drafting subcommittee.

• The platform committee report and any minority report would be prepared for public distribution and mailed to all convention delegates at least ten days before the convention opened.

• A minority report would be written upon the vote of 10 percent of the platform committee members present and voting at a meeting.

• All platform committee meetings would be open to the public.

The O'Hara Commission specifically rejected two proposals aimed at publicly committing presidential candidates on platform issues. One plan would have provided convention time for each contender to outline his or her views on the issues, answer questions from the floor, and make a final plea for the nomination. The other would have required the presidential and vice presidential nominees to pledge their wholehearted efforts to implement the platform recommendations. Presumably the commission considered the former proposal unseemly and the latter an unnecessary loyalty oath.

The major thrust of the recommendations that were approved was to make the platform committee more representative of the full convention and more responsive to the wishes of its members and other delegates in its operations. Certainly the new apportionment rule moved significantly toward similar constituencies for the committee and the convention as a whole. It also helped the more populous states, which previously had proportionately fewer votes in the committees than in the convention. The new rule assured at least the appearance of wider participation by the committee members, the delegates, and the public.

ABOLISHING THE PLATFORM

A more drastic alternative to reforming the platform would be to abolish it. Support for this suggestion is very scant; it is taken seriously by neither pragmatic politicians, who consider it too radical, nor scholars who think it might mean less attention to issues and intellect. But there have been nominating conventions that did not adopt platforms. The Liberal party of Canada in 1968 selected its leaders in such a convention, and debated public issues the next year at a national policy conference, where the discussion was not eclipsed by the nominating process.[26]

In terms of the voter's ability to evaluate the options rationally, eliminating the platform would mean that the voter would judge the candidates on the bases of their party affiliation, their individual records, and their statements during the campaign. Voters would not be distracted by a platform drafted by a party group whose members were not running for President. Yet there is no evidence that under present circumstances the voters *are* so distracted. The link between the public and the candidate is indisputably closer than the link between the public and the platform. More people remember Lyndon Johnson's campaign statement that American boys should not be sent to Vietnam to do what Asian boys ought to be doing than remember the Democratic platform of the same year that unequivocally pledged to support the

26. D. V. Smiley, "The National Party Leadership Convention in Canada: A Preliminary Analysis," *Canadian Journal of Political Science*, Vol. 1 (December 1968), pp. 387–90.

South Vietnamese in their struggle. Eliminating the platform would probably not affect substantially the process of voter choice.

The effect on bargaining at the convention would be more significant. Rather than eliminating the sort of sound and fury that the platform sometimes generates, its abolition would simply focus whatever factional disputes there were even more on the nominating process. Instead of less conflict there could be more, with increased urgency in the choice of the candidates and no platform to influence the winner and solace a Nelson Rockefeller or a Robert Taft. Even more than it has been in the past, the vice presidency might become a consolation prize.

Meanwhile, holding a separate convention after the election to discuss policy matters would not mean more disinterested deliberation. Political stakes are inherent in political debates. A successful candidate would undoubtedly have control over subsequent party policy conferences, whereas a candidate who had lost the election would be only one participant in the bargaining over party policy. Holding such a conference after the nomination but before the election would ensure the dominance of the nominee. Holding the meeting shortly before the nomination would simply transfer the jockeying by candidate factions to a different locale.

Since it is impossible to conduct a presidential campaign without *some* discussion of the issues, abolition of the platform would mean that the candidates would continue to develop their own policy statements. One way of doing this would be by writing their own platforms.

CANDIDATE PLATFORMS

More serious attention has been given to the proposal that each presidential aspirant develop his own detailed program, which automatically would be ratified by the party if that candidate were nominated. Proponents argue essentially that views on vital issues would be carefully, fully, and honestly elaborated by the candidate and considered as a package by the convention and the voters.

Candor, reason, and clarity of voter choice thereby would be promoted.[27]

Like the elimination of platforms, the adoption of candidate platforms would remove the statement of party principles as a separate object of bargaining among national leaders. As with the abolition option, all attention would be focused on the presidential and vice presidential nominations; minority factions might seize upon the latter as their only opportunity to win something. If so, the presidential nominee would have less freedom to select a running mate. Nonetheless, the vice presidential nominee would not necessarily be the person preferred by most of the delegates or the ordinary partisans.

Unlike the total elimination of the platform, however, the use of candidate platforms would ensure specific attention by the presidential aspirants' staffs to policy issues and perhaps would thereby facilitate a greater public identification of particular candidates with distinct views and recommendations. It could mean more issue-oriented campaigns, both in the race for the nomination and in the general election contest. Certainly it would not mean less attention to the issues.

Yet even today candidates have views that are known. Presidential races are not merely personality contests; every candidate produces innumerable position papers, and their stands on major issues are familiar to the attentive public. Since 1952 all the Republican and Democratic nominees have run on national party platforms that were at least fully acceptable to them, and were often their own specific recommendations.

What conceivably might change if platforms were drafted by the nominee's organization instead of by a committee is the specificity of the policies recommended; the approach might be more programmatic. If the candidates, particularly the nominees, took sharply defined positions on controversial issues, the effect on the

27. See, for example, Robert Walsh and Harvey Zeidenstein, "Replace Party Platforms with Candidate Platforms: A Modest Proposal for Reform," *Agora*, Vol. 1 (Fall 1969).

party might be divisive; those who disagreed might fail to support the nominees in the campaign. Even this would not represent an innovation; as Barry Goldwater learned, without candidate platforms as such, dissident partisans may abandon candidates with whom they strongly disagree.

The candidate who is elected would not necessarily be more likely to abide by the letter of his own platform than by that of the party's platform. The more specific the platform, the less the candidate would seem able to do so. Still, some candidates might feel more responsible for their own handiwork than for the product of a party committee.

Another uncertain issue would be the relationship between presidential and vice presidential nominees whose platforms had seriously differed. Would a balanced ticket involve subordinating the vice presidential nominee's views to those of the presidential candidate? Would the situation be very different from that when John Kennedy and Lyndon Johnson ran in tandem in 1960? The answers are uncertain. Given the strong tendency of politicians who are seeking to win elections to unite after even the bitterest of clashes, it seems likely that candidate platforms would not stand in the way of working alliances and would represent no major change from recent patterns.

NATIONAL COMMITTEE PLATFORMS

Another method that has been suggested for writing a party statement on the issues is for the national committee, a party council, or a similar organization, rather than a platform committee as such, to prepare a draft platform to be presented to the national convention, subject to amendment on the floor.

Clearly such a procedure would have the effect of strengthening one national arm of the party, and it would be a move in the direction of centrally controlled party government. The net change would not mean shifting decision-making to the national level, where it already takes place; it would give one group alone among national party leaders the privilege of drafting the platform. This would mean solidifying the status quo by strengthening the faction in control of the national committee (or its council) and hence weakening their opponents. It also would weaken the role of the candidates in years when the incumbent President was not running again. With the President running, the national committee would doubtless write whatever platform he wanted. In order to obtain a satisfactory platform, the candidates would be forced either to cultivate the committee members extensively or to take their issues to the floor. Thus the national committee platform would be the reverse of the candidate platform.

Any serious consideration of this idea calls for careful attention to the apportionment of the national committees. Like the platform committees until the Democrats' O'Hara Commission reform, these bodies do not reasonably reflect either party strength or the distribution of the national population. Nor do they mirror the apportionment of votes at the national conventions. This situation implies conflict over any platforms that are written by the national committee. Specifically, so long as the national committees continued to be apportioned on the basis of territorial sovereignty alone, the interests of small states and non-metropolitan areas would be overrepresented in population terms in the platform-drafting process, just as they are overrepresented in all formal deliberations of the national committees. At the same time, large-state and metropolitan interests would continue to carry considerable weight in the full conventions. Particularly because of the sensitivity and national importance of urban issues, this difference could mean more floor fights unless the candidates, the national committee chairman, and others intervened as they have in the past to head off such confrontations.

Not only would the presidential candidates, the congressional leaders, and the metropolitan interests stand to lose influence in drafting the platform; the contemporary reform movement would be thwarted as well. The reformers' objective in trying to improve conventions has been to give more power to rank-and-file partisans and ordinary delegates, rather than to "Establishment" organs like the national committees. If no one else took issues to the floor, the reformers surely would.

Frequent floor fights over the platform would not be bad in themselves. Issues would be fully aired before the public, and each faction would have an opportunity to be heard. Such a debate could also relieve tension and thereby serve a conciliatory purpose. Critical factors would be the extent of legitimacy ascribed to the decision-making process, the arena in which it took place, and thereby the ultimate decision itself. If belief in the fairness of procedures for writing and considering the platform were lacking, the debate would bring about more hostility than understanding. Such hostility would be a real threat in the case of national committee platforms because of the differences in constituency between the national committees and the full conventions.

MIDTERM ISSUES CONVENTION

Another persistent idea is that a national party convention should assemble every two years to thrash out the issues. As the aphorism has it, the cure for the ills of democracy is more democracy. In theory, a midterm convention would focus public attention between presidential elections on the major issues and the national leadership of the parties. It would help rejuvenate party enthusiasm by providing an opportunity for participation by the faithful and for an exchange of views aiming at a broad party consensus on public policy. Also it would bring ordinary partisans closer to the national leaders.

Yet it is also possible that a midterm convention would not be productive. Indeed, it might be counter-productive. The public, even party voters, might not be very much interested in what the leadership was doing between presidential campaigns; perhaps it takes a national race to generate widespread enthusiasm. A midterm convention might dim some of the luster of the presidential nominating convention. Alternatively, the public might not like what it saw. The debate over a midterm platform might stir up more conflict than consensus. Some members of Congress, as well as state and local spokesmen, would be certain to resent the project as an attempt to subordinate them to national party leadership. Prospective presidential candidates doubtless would use it as an opportunity to start their unofficial campaigns.

The character of the debate over a midterm platform would be affected significantly by whether the party was in or out of power. For the incumbents, the midterm convention typically would be what the convention traditionally has been—a forum for the expression of administration views and a demonstration of nationwide support. Very occasionally there would be major dissent within the party in power. Even then, the President would be almost certain to gain a vote of confidence from the convention. Although he might regard the struggle as an invasion of the presidential prerogative to establish party policy, he could benefit from the debate. While the insurgents would risk being revealed as simply a minority faction, they would be unlikely to turn down the opportunity to make their case and demonstrate real strength. Without the sort of mismanagement that damaged all factions of the Democratic party in 1968, the administration could explicate its policies, the insurgents could get a fair hearing, state and local partisans could participate in a national gathering, and the public would have an opportunity to benefit.

For the party out of power, the midterm convention would be still more important. It could provide a means to revive the party after its defeat in the presidential election. In addition to drafting a platform, it might consider issues of party governance and even select a national party leader. Whether it did or not, the midterm convention could clarify the presently confused leadership situation of the Out party. But such results are not guaranteed. If the party were nursing grievous injuries, as the Democrats were after 1968 and the Republicans after 1964, a midterm convention might come too early in the healing process and merely reopen old wounds. If the midterm convention took place in the summer, as the convention traditionally does, it would begin only a year and a half after all the unhappiness of an unsuccessful presidential campaign. While defeated parties are not always as divided and demoralized as in the cases mentioned, from time to time such a situation occurs. A mandatory midterm convention would be insufficiently flexible to work well under these circumstances.

Also, procedures for a midterm convention are uncertain. Methods of delegate selection, apportionment, and so on would have to be decided. Possibly state laws on primaries and conventions might have to be revised. Extensive planning, financing, and effort by politicians and their staffs would be needed. Even more than it is today, presidential politics would become a full-time occupation for large numbers of people.

Furthermore, a midterm convention—particularly one that also selected a party leader—would serve the interests of factions that were predominant in the party two years after the presidential election. Front-runners in the polls would presumably have more influence than other potential candidates. Known leaders would have an advantage over new faces. It is difficult to see, however, how the essential strategic situation would be different from that at the traditional convention. More generally, midterm conventions would give the Outs an opportunity to regroup and present a viable alternative to the government in power—to the benefit of the Outs and the Ins and the public at large.

All told, the idea is of sufficient merit to deserve testing. One way would be for the parties to experiment with a midterm meeting without committing themselves to continuing the practice. If it worked, it could be tried again; if it did not, it could be abandoned.

Considerable experimentation with the platform-writing process has taken place during the past two decades; continued experimenting is altogether desirable because of the importance of the document in presidential politics. The platform is the means by which all the party's presidential candidates influence the views of the party, by which a party consensus influences the views of the nominee, and by which both influence what the presidential nominee does if elected.

Although some have accepted the significance of the platform, few citizens have read it—let alone participated in writing it. A national or even a partywide referendum on the platform would be impossible; authoritative statements on the issues must be drafted by the relatively small group of people who have some understanding of the issues and their implications for the party, the government, and the citizens.

Yet there are means—some that have already been used, others that have merely been suggested—for encouraging wide participation in making the platform. Both parties have tried to give an increased opportunity to all who want to express their views by holding regional platform hearings. Platform committee members and staff should take account of these views in drafting the party statement. In recent years, the staffs and committee members have made increasing use of various party documents that establish continuity in policy and ensure consideration of a wide spectrum of party opinion in platform deliberations.

Presidential candidates, through their staffs, should be involved directly in writing the platforms. In this, most Republican nominees have played a greater role than have their Democratic counterparts. The O'Hara Commission recommendation that each candidate have a non-voting representative on the platform committee is a structural change designed to assure that each candidate's views get a fair hearing and the winner's views are linked more emphatically with those of the party consensus. Since the platforms in recent times have been at least acceptable to the candidates, there is every reason why the nominees should stress them more in trying to build a popular coalition during the campaign, and the winning candidate should emphasize platform pledges in rallying national support for the presidential program.

Ordinary delegates should have the opportunity to make a rational decision in voting for or against the platform committee report. Usually their votes have been based on the views of their state delegation chairman, their representatives on the platform committee, the attitudes of the presidential candidate they favor, the platform presentation and floor debate if any, and similar cues. Insofar as it is feasible—and those who have taken part in platform committee operations seem to agree that it can be done—the delegates should have an opportunity to read the platform document before the floor vote and make an independent judgment if they wish.

Finally, for purposes of public education, the platform should be more widely discussed and copies or at least summaries made more readily available. The national committees long have given copies to those seeking them; state and local party organizations should do the same. More specific attention to the platform by the candidates could provoke a wider public interest. The news media could focus more attention on the platforms, perhaps by analyzing the similarities and differences between the two major parties during the campaign as well as those of the major party factions at the time of the convention. All of these suggestions are intended to provoke the widest possible discussion of major issues during the presidential campaign.

Chapter Six

☆

THE PRESS, THE PUBLIC, AND THE POLITICIANS

Some kinds of communications, on some kinds of issues,
brought to the attention of some kinds of people under some kinds of conditions,
have some kinds of effects.
Bernard Berelson

ALTHOUGH IT IS OBVIOUS THAT news coverage of the political party convention in some way affects its public image, no one knows just how. But it *is* known that in 1968 some commentators charged that the Democratic convention was "controlled" to repress the insurgent views of ordinary partisans and delegates; and the Democrats lost the election. In 1964 some commentators insisted on pointing out that Barry Goldwater was being nominated by the convention at a time when moderate Republicans led him in the opinion polls; and the Republicans lost. Those two elections sufficed to make press coverage a central topic in the discussion about democracy, fairness, and especially legitimacy at the conventions. (The term "press," as used here, includes the electronic news media as well as the traditional printed media.) Clearly the press is the middleman in the mysterious transactions between political leaders and the public. Hence the fairness with which the news media are treated is of central concern in any assessment of convention procedures. Moreover, because of television, conventions must not only *be* fair, they also must *look* fair.

The Press and the Public

Television is today the primary source of news. An increasingly important source as the number of TV sets in use grew rapidly during the 1950s, by 1963 television had surpassed the newspapers and other media. A November 1968 Roper poll found that 65 percent of the respondents became best acquainted with national candidates through television; 24 percent through newspapers; 4 percent, radio; 5 percent, magazines; 4 percent, personal communications; and 2 percent, other sources.[1]

According to the Nielsen ratings of the conventions from 1952 through 1968, between 20 and 30 percent of the potential television audience was watching during an average minute—a better-than-average combined rating for all of the various categories of television programs, but individually less than the usual audience for single prime time network broadcasts.[2] Peak convention viewing came at moments of greatest political drama; in 1960, for the two parties, these were when Senator Eugene McCarthy nominated Adlai Stevenson (seen in twenty million homes—44 percent of all households with television) and Vice President Richard Nixon gave his acceptance speech (38 percent of television households). The latter was consciously scheduled for a time when a maximum viewing audience was available. Yet both peaks of convention viewing were surpassed that year by the television audience for the first Kennedy-Nixon debate, with presumably a bipartisan and hence larger audience; it was seen in thirty million homes (66 percent of the TV households).[3] Still, it is worth noting that 49 per-

1. Burns W. Roper, "A Ten-Year View of Public Attitudes toward Television and Other Mass Media, 1959–1968" (New York: Television Information Office, 1969), pp. 2, 9.

2. Television convention audience estimates for 1952–68, courtesy of the A. C. Nielsen Company; average 1968 Nielsen ratings for different types of shows are found in Jack Lyle, "Contemporary Functions of the Mass Media," in U.S. National Commission on the Causes and Prevention of Violence, *Mass Media and Violence* (Government Printing Office, 1969), p. 209.

3. Cited in Charles A. H. Thomson, "Mass Media Activities and Influence," in Paul T. David (ed.), *The Presidential Election and Transition 1960–1961* (Brookings Institution, 1961), pp. 96, 99.

cent of homes with television in 1952 watched Nixon's "Checkers" speech on a single network.[4] Many viewers would prefer to watch programs other than conventions; according to one survey in New York City, which has more stations than any other area, 55 percent of the viewers were tuned in to programs other than the 1964 Republican convention. Most of them were watching a Yankees-Orioles baseball game or an Elvis Presley movie.[5]

"Perhaps the place to start looking for a credibility gap," observed Spiro T. Agnew in a now legendary speech on television news coverage, "is not in the offices of the Government in Washington but in the studios of the [television] networks in New York."[6] In the same speech the Vice President charged also that "the news that 40 million Americans receive each night is determined by a handful of men responsible only to their corporate employers and is filtered through a handful of commentators who admit to their own set of biases."[7]

The impact of media coverage of the convention is presumably affected by the extent to which the public believes what it reads, hears, and sees in the news. No one knows how many of his fellow citizens agree with Agnew's viewpoint. There is sound evidence, however, that many who watched the 1968 Democratic convention did not believe what the press told them about it. While most reporters described the treatment of demonstrators by the Chicago police as excessively violent, the public overwhelmingly disagreed. The Columbia Broadcasting System (CBS) reported that its mail was running 11 to 1 unfavorable to its correspondents' coverage. A *New York Times* telephone survey taken the day after the Chicago disorders found a landslide of support for the police. And 57 percent of the respondents in a nationwide survey by the University of Michigan's Survey Research Center (SRC) said either that

4. Charles A. H. Thomson, *Television and Presidential Politics* (Brookings Institution, 1956), p. 57.

5. *New York Times*, Aug. 15, 1964, p. 72.

6. Speech to Mid-West Regional Republican Committee, Des Moines, Iowa, Nov. 13, 1969; reprinted in *Vital Speeches*, Vol. 36 (Dec. 1, 1969), p. 100.

7. *Ibid.*, pp. 99–100.

the police had used the right amount of force (32 percent) or that they had not used enough force (25 percent). Only 19 percent in the SRC survey agreed with most reporters that too much force had been used.[8] In a poll sponsored by *Newsweek* two years later, the Chicago convention was one of the major news stories most often mentioned as an example of journalistic misinterpretation.[9]

Probably the reaction to coverage of the Chicago convention is not a reliable indication of public belief in the news media, at conventions or elsewhere. Yet considerable skepticism about the media is reflected in a more inclusive group of surveys, recently collected from polls taken since the 1930s.[10] These polls are difficult to interpret as a group because many are old and the questions have varied. None deals specifically with conventions. However, the answers to thirty-four of these survey questions are intriguing in what they suggest about the extent of public belief in the fairness, impartiality, truthfulness, or accuracy of the various media on politics and public issues. Until 1960 the vast majority of those polled considered that the media were fair in their judgments. Since then the public has become much more critical. In recent years television news has been trusted by the public more than other media; newspapers have been low in public esteem. This trend is substantiated by the Roper data shown in Table 6-1. Television has been growing in public confidence while newspapers have been declining.

Still, public skepticism of the news media should not be overstated. People turn to the media and the commentators that they trust most. Much may depend upon the wording of questions in the polls. The November 1970 *Newsweek* poll showed that those who actually use each of the various media have more confidence in them than the data in Table 6-1 would suggest. The *Newsweek* poll, taken by the Gallup organization with no indication to the

8. John P. Robinson, "Public Reaction to Political Protest: Chicago 1968," *Public Opinion Quarterly*, Vol. 34 (Spring 1970), pp. 1–2.

9. "The People and the Press," *Newsweek*, Vol. 76 (Nov. 9, 1970), p. 23.

10. Hazel Erskine, "The Polls: Opinion of the News Media," *Public Opinion Quarterly*, Vol. 34 (Winter 1970–71), pp. 630–43.

TABLE 6-1. *Medium That Would Be Believed in Case of Conflicting Reports, 1959–68*
Percent

Year	Television	Newspapers	Radio	Magazines	Don't know/ no answer
1959	29	32	12	10	17
1961	39	24	12	10	17
1963	36	24	12	10	18
1964	41	23	8	10	18
1968	44	21	8	11	16

Source: Burns W. Roper, "A Ten-Year View of Public Attitudes Toward Television and Other Mass Media, 1959–1968" (Television Information Office, 1969), p. 4.

respondents that a news magazine was sponsoring it, showed that vast majorities of regular newspaper readers, TV news viewers, magazine readers, and radio news listeners thought that their media were doing an "excellent" or "good" job of keeping the public informed. "Poor" ratings were less than 10 percent of the total for each of the media.[11]

The image of political events that comes to the public through the news media is necessarily different from an all-encompassing view of the situation. Any explanation of what is going on is inherently selective. The sociologists Kurt and Gladys Lang, who have studied this phenomenon in several experiments, conclude that "television, as well as radio and print, always introduces some element of refraction into the actuality it conveys."[12]

In other words, the news media change the image of an event just as a prism changes the image of a ray of light passing through it. But how? One way is simply that reporters try to make the conventions and other political events more dramatic than they actually are. In this sense, television and the other news media reflect journalistic values about what "news" is. Studying crowd reaction to a parade for General Douglas MacArthur in 1951, the Langs found that: "Compared with the spectator's experience of

11. "The People and the Press," p. 22.
12. *Politics and Television* (Quadrangle Books, 1968), p. 290.

extended boredom and sore feet, alleviated only by a brief glimpse of the hero of the day, his previous experiences over television had seemed truly exciting and promised even greater 'sharing of excitement' *if only one were present.*"[13] Many who stood and watched the MacArthur parade said they would have preferred to view it on television.

Beyond injecting added excitement into the proceedings, television news explains and sometimes predicts convention events, thus giving the viewer the sense of actually being in the audience of a drama that is created by the material that television presents to the viewer. Today, the Langs assert, the television audience is so vast that the televised event itself "becomes the actuality. It is subsequently talked about, written about, and critically evaluated. . . ."[14] For the public, the televised event may give such an illusion of realism that all things appear either known or concealed. In the Langs' observations of televiewers, the successful broadcasting of fairly simple events like speeches meant that the less successful broadcasting of complex events like state caucuses confused many viewers; when they could not see exactly what was transpiring, many leapt to the conclusion that important decisions were being made and concealed in smoke-filled rooms.[15]

The most serious charge of this order is that the news media consciously distort the information disseminated to the public. Since a random sample of journalists would doubtless turn up about as much human fallibility and venality as would a survey of any comparable sector of the population, systematically biased presentations of the news are possible. Biased news coverage presented as truth could seriously impair the capacity of the public to understand public affairs. However, one of the basic credos of journalism is that there should be a high wall of separation between the presentation of facts and of opinions. David Brinkley of NBC News often pointedly says that what he is expressing is

13. *Ibid.*, p. 47.
14. *Ibid.*, p. 297.
15. *Ibid.*, pp. 300–304.

simply his own viewpoint. In addition, political leaders are free to try, just as Vice President Agnew has, to refute statements in the news media to which they take exception. There are also libel laws. Beyond that, the major safeguard against misleading news coverage must be the good judgment of individual citizens.

The skepticism about the media that is reflected in the polls suggests that the public is aware of the possibility of news distortion; and the political implication of this awareness is intriguing. What happens when people don't believe what the press tells them about politics? Again, no one knows. One hypothesis is that the public turns against the protagonists of the political drama it sees. Both Richard Nixon and Hubert Humphrey reportedly believe that the Chicago convention effectively decided the 1968 presidential election by alienating many voters from the unruly Democrats. Humphrey says he is convinced that the late date of the Democratic convention made it virtually impossible for him to catch up the ground he lost as a result of what happened in Chicago. Coverage of the police appears to have turned many viewers against the news media. Another theory is that the skeptical public simply exercises more or less rational judgment among the competing points of view—accepting and rejecting what the press tells them as it does what politicians and other people tell them, on the basis principally of prior personal background and experience. If this were the case, a healthy dose of public skepticism about the news media and about politicians would foster maximum public understanding of, and involvement in, the convention process.

The preceding analysis shows that available data dealing with the influence of the news media on public attitudes are not scientifically conclusive. Although there is no clearly established relationship between press coverage and voting behavior, party leaders have found the political stakes too high to leave to chance. The convention traditionally has been the beginning of the election campaign. The image of the party and of its candidates is powerfully projected at the national party gathering. Accordingly, politicians have tried to arrange conventions so as to present their party, their candidates, and their views in the most favorable light possible.

The Impact on Conventions

While it has not brought about the millennium of a consistently newsworthy, entertaining, efficient, and politically satisfactory convention, the presence of the news media has changed the way in which the institution operates. Exposing convention proceedings to a mass television audience beginning in 1952 has made politicians much more conscious of the appearance of their actions and hence sensitive to issues of fairness in procedure. Thus television was an instrumental factor in the 1952 Republican fight over the fair play amendment, the credentials challenge of the Mississippi Freedom Democrats in 1964, and the allegations of elite control made by the anti-Johnson Democrats in 1968. Factions believing that the substance or administration of a convention rule discriminated against them have not hesitated to take their case to the news media; realizing this, those in charge of carrying out the rules have sought to avoid criticisms on these grounds. In this sense, television (and, to a lesser extent, the other news media) served as an ally of the new critics of conventions.

Other changes wrought by the news media have been managerial. Site selection, for example, now must be negotiated by the parties in consultation with the television networks, whose tons of equipment and hundreds of employees must be accommodated. There is no evidence, however, that a convention city has ever been chosen specifically because of the needs of television. Indeed, the two parties nearly always have rejected the networks' pleas to hold their conventions in the same place; not since both parties met at Chicago in 1952 has a common city been selected. Nonetheless, the needs of the electronic and other media have added a new dimension to the choice of a site. In 1952 the International Amphitheater was used as the convention hall, instead of the

Chicago Stadium as was originally planned, because the stadium lacked adequate space for television broadcasting. And in 1968 the needs of television provided the most powerful argument against moving the Democratic convention when it became clear that Chicago would be the scene of dangerous confrontations.

The scheduling, agenda, and rules of conventions also have changed significantly since the advent of national television. Important events are scheduled either to exploit prime television time—as in the case of speeches by popular party figures—or to avoid it—as with the Democrats' bitter Vietnam debate in 1968. The time allotted for most speeches, demonstrations, presentations, and other ceremonial events has been reduced greatly. The polling of delegations, once commonplace, has become rare. There are fewer roll call votes; Adlai Stevenson in 1952 was the last presidential candidate to have been nominated after the first ballot. In keeping with these innovations, recent conventions have been much shorter, as Table 6-2 shows. A repetition is unlikely of the

TABLE 6-2. *Number of Sessions and Duration of the Major Party National Conventions, 1952–68*

Year	Number of sessions	Time elapsed
1952		
Democrats	10	47 hours, 10 minutes
Republicans	10	41 hours, 1 minute
1956		
Democrats	9	31 hours, 39 minutes
Republicans	5	18 hours
1960		
Democrats	5	27 hours, 55 minutes
Republicans	5	18 hours
1964		
Democrats	4	14 hours, 31 minutes
Republicans	5	26 hours, 55 minutes
1968		
Democrats	5	28 hours, 48 minutes
Republicans	5	23 hours, 40 minutes

Sources: Republican National Committee; and official proceedings of Democratic national conventions.

marathon 1924 Democratic convention, which lasted nearly three weeks and required 103 ballots to nominate a presidential candidate. Furthermore, the credentials and platform committees now meet before the convention opens, thus expediting convention week business.

The theatrical aspects of television have had further implications. Broadcasting executives have served as convention directors for both parties. Old-style orators have been replaced by more telegenic personalities, selected to enhance the party image. Delegates have been urged to be in their seats, to look attentive, and to avoid any stunts that would make the party appear foolish.

Television itself has become a major internal communications network. It is the best way for people at the convention to keep up with what is going on. Some delegates have brought TV sets to their seats; others question reporters. The news media, particularly television, are used strategically. Edward Kennedy's rumored presidential candidacy in 1968 was reported by Sander Vanocur of the National Broadcasting Company (NBC); John Chancellor of the same network effectively squelched the reports. Reporters for the printed media feel that they have been demoted to second-class rank by the celebrity status of television correspondents; though sometimes resentful, they are unable to retaliate.

Increasingly elaborate staging of televised conventions may have affected the decision-making process. The conventional wisdom about open covenants openly arrived at has it that the presence of the press encourages candor, honesty, and greater concern for the public interest. But it may simply move decision-making from public forums into private rooms. Politicians usually prefer to hold important consultations outside the reach of most reporters. It is not that political leaders want to deceive the public, but they need some privacy to protect themselves from the opposition. As reporters have become more nearly ubiquitous in the convention hall, committee rooms, and state caucuses, these sessions increasingly have served only to enact formally what has already been decided elsewhere. The major exceptions to exclusion of the news media from decision-making sessions occur because politicians are unwilling to deny access to a reporter of the stature, say, of Walter Cronkite; and because some journalists are so politicized that they have become confidants of candidates and their staffs.

A crucial question, of course, is whether coverage by the news media has influenced the choice of a nominee. The assertion frequently made that the media, particularly television, promote the success of candidates who have a sparkling public image and perhaps little else is difficult to test. Certainly a favorable public image has never hurt. No ideal television candidate, however, has emerged and been nominated. John Kennedy's good looks undoubtedly helped, but it took him time to master effective television speaking. The appearance of Richard Nixon—who ironically was considered in 1952 an image of youthful vigor that contrasted well with his running mate's age and experience—may have hurt Nixon in 1960; but his party nominated him for President twice and once succeeded in electing him. Dwight Eisenhower's managers used television in 1952 to open up credentials committee hearings, much to the advantage of their candidate; but it seems reasonable to believe that Eisenhower would have won the nomination anyway. Being telegenic is not in itself a guarantee of victory. George Romney, Henry Cabot Lodge, William Scranton, Mark Hatfield, and Eugene McCarthy never have been selected as their parties' presidential nominee. Some observers have suggested that national television helps senators and hurts governors as presidential candidates, since the former have better access to the Washington press.[16] The nomination of more senators (and vice presidents) than governors since 1952 lends credence to this theory, although the increasing importance for presidential candidates of experience in foreign affairs may be a more significant

16. Malcolm Moos, "New Light on the Nominating Process," in Stephen K. Bailey (ed.), *Research Frontiers in Politics and Government* (Brookings Institution, 1955), p. 156.

reason for this pattern. On the whole, though, political leaders at conventions have more to do than contemplate the media personalities of their candidates. Many, for example, are absorbed in cultivating individual journalists.

The Press and the Politicians

Throughout the political system party leaders and representatives of the press regard each other warily. Writing of public officials and the news media, Francis E. Rourke has likened their relationship to a system of exchange:

> Officials trade information to reporters in return for publicity. But neither side is content with the resources offered in exchange by the other. Reporters seek access to information that officials would prefer to conceal, and officials attempt to obtain more favorable publicity than reporters are willing to provide.[17]

Each has potential sanctions against the others. Reporters may reveal, or threaten to reveal, what politicians do not want known; politicians may shut off, or threaten to shut off, valuable news sources.[18] Yet each side needs the other; and after some experience in doing business together, each understands the other better. Conflict is less common than cooperation. As already noted, some journalists and politicians become friends and allies. A more serious problem of the typical exchange system, as Rourke points out (and of the friend-and-ally situation as well), is the disregard of the interests of the public in obtaining adequate information about what political leaders are doing.

Occasional conflicts between politicians and the news media have sparked public controversy. Sometimes the politicians *and* the press *and* the public are dissatisfied with the system of exchanging information for publicity. Such melodramatic clashes as

17. In a review of Delmer D. Dunn, *Public Officials and the Press* (Addison-Wesley Publishing Co., 1969) in *Administrative Science Quarterly*, Vol. 15 (June 1970), p. 257.

18. On the latter, see John Rothchild, "The Stories Reporters Don't Write," *The Washington Monthly*, Vol. 3 (June 1971), pp. 20–27.

those at the 1964 Republican convention, when John Chancellor of NBC News was arrested and marched off by sheriff's deputies because he refused to leave the convention floor and former President Eisenhower inveighed against "sensation-seeking columnists and commentators who couldn't care less about the good of our party,"[19] transcend their momentary entertainment value. They symbolize the conflicting interests and objectives in transmitting the public image of conventions.

Inherent strains in the relationship between political leaders and the news media are further complicated by the differing interests among politicians and among the media. As conflict is at the heart of politics, so competition is a cardinal principle of journalism. While everyone seeks "good" press coverage of the conventions, what is good for the Democratic National Committee is not necessarily good for Hubert Humphrey or the New Mobilization Committee to End the War in Vietnam, let alone the citizenry. And what is good for NBC is not necessarily good for CBS or the *Denver Post*.

Three kinds of political leaders deal with the news media at national conventions: convention planners and managers, candidate organizations, and interest group spokesmen. For all of them, the convention represents the supreme test of their capability and achievement. Convention planners and managers—the national chairman, the committee on arrangements, the site selection committee, and the national committee staff—offer access to the convention and facilities for covering it in exchange for publicity that they hope will reflect favorably on their party and themselves. They must constantly balance the claims of the press, however, with competing interests—efficiency of operations, good public relations, fairness to all seeking legitimate access, and responsiveness to party leaders—particularly the President in the case of the party in power.

In their exchanges with the press, candidate organizations trade

19. *Official Report of the Proceedings of the Republican National Convention, 1964* (Republican National Committee, 1966), p. 185.

access to a presidential hopeful for publicity about their effort. But strategies may differ. Apparently candidates seeking to demonstrate widespread popular support—an Eisenhower, a Rockefeller, or the Kennedys—are more accessible than candidates trying to win by emphasizing the inside route of party organizations—a Taft, a Nixon, or a Goldwater. Also some candidates simply have more natural rapport with journalists than do others. If they enjoy this advantage, their managers will try to exploit it; if not, they will try to minimize contacts with the media.

Political groups other than those explicitly supporting a candidate trade information for publicity about their cause. Recently the most notable groups have been those involved in the civil rights movement and the peace movement. Both have seized upon the conventions as occasions for presenting their message—most dramatically through demonstrations, most traditionally through platform debates. At the 1964 Democratic convention, civil rights strategists used a new tactic, rightly judging that their objectives would be furthered by the publicity resulting from credentials contests. As has already been noted, however, the confrontations of the peace forces with the Chicago authorities four years later were counterproductive for the demonstrators in terms of public opinion.[20]

For reporters, conventions are a great news source—a quadrennial combination of the World Series and the All-Star game. For those who cover presidential politics, conventions are nearly as important as they are to the candidates and campaign workers; by the time the convention opens, they have been writing about the forthcoming election for several years.

Eric Sevareid has said: "You can get the ratings, or the critical plaudits, or both, but you better get one."[21] Whatever medium of expression is used, the ancient journalistic dictum applies: "Get it first and get it right." Both the impulse to scoop and the impulse to understand cause journalists at a fast-moving convention (and

20. Robinson, "Public Reaction to Political Protest," pp. 1–9.
21. Quoted by Charles McDowell, Jr., of the *Richmond Times-Dispatch.*

perhaps even more at a slow-moving convention) to be constantly in search of a new angle, a new source, a new picture, a new perspective, a new development.[22]

Each of the news media also has its special concerns. Each has a particular audience, which serves much the same function as does a politician's constituency. The most important medium to the public and the politicians, and perhaps even to the grudging press corps, is national television.[23] Conventions, like the counting of returns on election night, provide dramatic events that are especially suitable for television broadcasting—even though little of the most important convention business is visible. The television industry, particularly the network news departments, is highly competitive. And the conventions are a prime indicator of how well the news departments are doing—compared with one another, with other divisions of their own networks, with past years, and with other news department programs.

Unlike printed journalism, television's fundamental unit is time rather than space; it transmits its message through sight and sound rather than through words on a page; and it has a huge audience that is accustomed to spending much of its leisure time watching television. Television is often described as more intimate than other media, more capable of giving its viewers the illusion that they are actually present at the event being broadcast. It performs better at transmitting experiences felt than at communicating facts or analysis; viewers may feel that they are present at a convention but have little real understanding of what is happening. Moreover,

22. Delmer D. Dunn has also noted that a reporter may play and perceive himself as playing any or all of the following roles: neutral information transmitter, translator and interpreter of political events to the people, representative of the public, and participant in the events that occur. See Dunn's *Public Officials and the Press* (Addison-Wesley Publishing Co., 1969), pp. 7–18. David S. Broder has described the press that follows presidential politics as composed of summarizers, talent scouts, handicappers, and public defenders. "Political Reporters in Presidential Politics," *The Washington Monthly*, Vol. 1 (February 1969), pp. 20–33.

23. Some independent radio and television stations and groups also cover the conventions. They have contended that they are often ignored by convention officials because of the emphasis on network coverage.

television is at its best when its pictures and its words "reinforce each other";[24] if they do not, the message may be muted. When decisions are made as to which news stories should be run, those that fit television's production needs better are preferred. Finally, because television's convention coverage is hectic and prolonged, commentators must make instant evaluations without adequate time for careful assessment, some material is broadcast only to fill air time, and sometimes sensation takes preference over significance.[25]

The composition of a television network's production crew further distinguishes its coverage from that of the printed press. The televiewer sees a favorite anchor man and his colleagues—familiar and trusted faces and experienced journalists. Yet in a sense they are merely actors in a performance where the important decisions are made by a producer. It is the producer who decides which among the available images flickers on the home screens from minute to minute. This involves split-second choices among pressures from reporters, sponsors, technicians, political factions, and the competition. It also means heavy reliance on the producer's judgment. Some producers have been trained as journalists; others are professional television specialists rather than professional newsmen; thus, they may emphasize drama more than news— although this does not necessarily make them either more or less fair in their judgments than a newspaper editor, for example, would be with the same material.

Beginning in 1924, radio has brought the conventions to the attentive public as well as to a new audience of those who have not regularly followed politics in the printed media; today radio covers the conventions more thoroughly than it did in the 1920s and reaches many people who do not watch television. Although it lacks television's commanding visual appeal, radio is more suited

24. John Whale, *The Half-Shut Eye: Television and Politics in Britain and America* (Macmillan and St. Martin's Press, 1969), p. 24.

25. See the testimony by Neil Hickey of *TV Guide* before the Democratic National Committee's Commission on Rules, July 26, 1969, reprinted in *TV Guide*, Vol. 17 (Sept. 6, 1969), p. 9.

to the spoken word, which still dominates the convention format. Otherwise, it is similar in many ways to television, particularly in the network structure and in heavy dependence on technology.

A great variety of printed news media cover the conventions: wire services, newspaper chains and groups, individual papers, periodicals, newsletters, and the trade press. One major difference among them is the speed with which they disseminate the news. Because television and radio offer instantaneous communication, the written media concentrate less on bulletins and more on interpretive depth at conventions, as they do elsewhere. Wire services like the Associated Press (AP) and United Press International (UPI), which are concerned primarily with getting facts as quickly as possible to their several thousand subscribers, fall somewhere between the electronic media with their "you are there" emphasis and the journals that are less obsessed with time. At the opposite pole from television and radio news lies the periodical press, with its relatively leisurely deadlines. Another important distinction is that of focus. Some reporters cover the national denouement of who will be nominated; far more follow "regional" stories about particular state delegations. The former roam among candidate groups and other sources of news about the candidates; regional reporters virtually live with their delegations, often staying at the same hotel and taking meals with them. Finally, there are major structural differences. The *New York Times* and other large papers have many reporters, each covering a particular convention story. Far more typical is the one-person operation, with a single reporter responsible for searching out stories of interest to a particular set of readers. Representatives of the larger papers are more influential in national politics; reporters for smaller papers are more common at the conventions.

Issues and Alternatives

When the convention brings together party leaders and representatives of the press—all seeking in idiosyncratic ways to educate the public—there results a babel of more or less strident voices, occasionally angry outbursts, a torrent of public information, and some persistent questions about the place of the news media on such occasions. Television is often singled out for criticism, or at least discussion, because it has the largest audiences, the largest convention staffs, and untold cubic feet of paraphernalia that often get in the way of politicians and other journalists. In truth, the issues involved concern all the media, not the least because the fate of television news affects the character of coverage by everyone else.

EXTENT OF COVERAGE

There is no serious complaint about the fact that reporters are virtually ubiquitous at conventions and send out reams of copy; the real issue is the length of television programming. Which is preferable—extended coverage, nightly summaries, or some combination of the two?

Massive press coverage of the conventions was long believed to serve the interests of both the parties and the press. Party leaders tended to equate maximum news coverage with maximum publicity for the party and its candidates. After 1964 and 1968 they became aware of the fine line between publicity and notoriety. The news media also long have followed conventions to the point of obsession; they too have come to understand that covering the conventions occasionally can net them little more than a black eye—figuratively or literally.

When the national television networks began broadcasting the conventions, they at first covered the formal sessions from the opening rap of the gavel until the end. But the scope was extended quickly. Beginning in 1952, at every convention, every network— with the sole exception of the American Broadcasting Company (ABC) in 1968—has been on the air for a longer period than the duration of the formal sessions. In 1968, ABC shifted to nightly summaries of major events. Although its aim had been to save money, its ratings soared; hence the third of the three networks will continue its new format in 1972. \

The traditional format focuses the efforts of the television news departments on the convention shows in an all-out test of relative mettle. It is a big chance for the news departments and a great opportunity to exploit the competitive instincts of the networks and the reporters, presumably to public advantage. Yet it may provide them with stimulation at the cost of other television news programs that might have been aired had not such expensive resources been used on the conventions. How many other television news projects have been shelved because the conventions took priority? No one knows, or at least no one is telling. Again, the present system provides political leaders with a windfall of free publicity. At the same time, it has meant substantial intrusion into the decision-making process. As for the public, it gets the most extended view through elongated convention coverage; it does not necessarily thereby obtain the most coherent, accurate, incisive, or interesting account of events.

The shorter summary format adopted by ABC in 1968 has quite different implications. For the networks, it is cheaper—a boon for the less wealthy and an opportunity for the more affluent to undertake additional television news programs. It may mean missing some scoops, which violates a journalistic ethic; but there are few truly memorable scoops at conventions. It means entrusting producers and reporters with more leeway for exercising news judgment in summarizing the day's events. In the right situation, this could mean journalism of better quality for each dollar spent; but this is not assured automatically.

For political leaders, shorter convention coverage would entail less intrusion into their activities. Though the networks might have the same access, presumably they would reduce their activities somewhat because they actually would need less material. However, it need not follow that the electronic journalists would stress the events that the parties wanted the public to see. If they did not, convention managers might be inclined to streamline their production to regain attention lost because of boredom or inadequate news value.

For the public, shorter television coverage of the conventions would be less panoramic and more pithy. During the hours when the convention was not on the air, regular programs would be broadcast. And when the convention was being broadcast, the show might be more interesting. ABC's Nielsen ratings suggest the better viewer response: only 2.2 percent to 3.7 percent of the potential television audience for the Republican convention was watching during the years 1952–64; but 7.7 percent watched the convention when the coverage was shorter in 1968; from 2.3 percent to 4.3 percent of the potential television audience viewed the Democratic conventions during the years 1952–64, but 8.5 percent watched when the coverage was shorter in 1968.[26]

With three commercial networks, an educational network, and many independent stations and groups all covering the conventions, a strong case can be made for *variety* in the extent to which they broadcast convention events. There is a small, attentive public that is fascinated by marathon coverage. A much larger audience will watch whichever show seems livelier; their decision may depend on the identity of the network's anchor men, or it may be influenced by the amount of time and effort required to understand the convention story as portrayed by the various networks; or it may favor a program with more analysis and clash of views.

The networks, because of their competitive nature, are unlikely to decide jointly who will cover what. Although there has been some pool camera coverage for all networks, each has sought to outdo the others in supplementing it. The networks also are sensitive to charges that they manage the news. However, though it is probably idle to speculate on what effects such a collaboration might cause, it is nevertheless interesting. For instance, the enormous savings involved might well result in an upgrading in the overall quality of the coverage. With direct rating competition eliminated, flamboyant handling of various aspects of the convention would be unnecessary, and objectivity might be enhanced; and since back-to-back comparison of the networks would be available without dial-switching, each network might be doubly eager to be

26. Television audience estimates courtesy A. C. Nielsen Company.

at its best. Furthermore, having responsibility for only one-third of the coverage would surely give each network an opportunity for deeper analysis of much that now receives only cursory attention. And with pooled facilities, it would be relatively inexpensive for affiliated stations to tape insert summaries of the news most vital to their individual constituencies and place them in regularly scheduled breaks (such as the local 11 o'clock news) without destroying the national scope of the coverage. Convention managers and delegates too might be glad to have only one set of television lights, cameras, and technicians outside the caucus room door instead of three or more.

In any case, with the apparent success of ABC in 1968, deviation from the norm of hyper-extended coverage has been encouraged. This trend could mean more innovation in television journalism generally—a move that many in the news business and outside it would applaud.

ARRANGEMENTS FOR COVERAGE

Traditionally there has been considerable give and take between convention managers and the press over the physical arrangements for newsmen—particularly space in the hall and passes to the floor. In 1952 far more elaborate arrangements had to be made for television. Although occasional conflicts arose, the working assumption was that the exchange of adequate facilities for good publicity was mutually advantageous. Since the potential dysfunctions of news coverage have become manifest, however, even trivialities of arrangements have assumed the proportions of confrontations on principle.

Generally the convention planners and managers, in consultation with media representatives, have chosen a location with hotel rooms, transportation, work space, and communications systems that are considered adequate for the press; they then have turned detailed arrangements over to the media themselves. Thus the parties decide how many representatives of the media can be accommodated over all; there were 7,000 in 1968.[27] The elected representatives of the news media in the congressional press galleries supervise accreditation of, and arrangements for, members of the press. This has meant one less distasteful job for the convention managers, and for the news media it has meant decision-making by their peers.

By far the largest operation is the television network production, which cost in 1968 up to $5 million each for CBS and NBC and somewhat less for the shorter ABC coverage.[28] Most of the huge outlays go for salaries, equipment, and transportation. CBS alone sent about 800 people and 200 tons of equipment to Miami Beach and to Chicago, where it built an anchor booth, two studios, and a newsroom to supplement its mobile facilities.[29] Its staff in 1964 was estimated to be about half editorial, with "about eight technicians and four producers to every on-the-air reporter."[30] Only part of the costs are recouped through commercial sponsorship.

By and large, convention arrangements for the press have worked smoothly. The chief irritation for convention managers has been that the news media demand an unreasonable number of passes, an issue that was dealt with in Chapter 4. Except for occasional complaints about mixups in hotel reservations, overloaded switchboards, too few taxicabs, too many traffic jams, and other essentially minor irritations, the press has generally been satisfied.

Reporters did lament, however, that in 1968, the Democrats failed to plan as far in advance as the press, particularly the networks, would have liked, and that the news media were not adequately informed about arrangements for coverage. The peculiar chaos of the Democratic party in mid-1968 was the principal cause

27. Republican National Committee estimate.
28. Charles McDowell, Jr., "Carnival of Excess: TV at the Conventions," *Atlantic*, Vol. 222 (July 1968), p. 40.
29. Thomas Whiteside, "Corridor of Mirrors: The Television Editorial Process, Chicago," *Columbia Journalism Review*, Vol. 4 (Winter 1968/1969), p. 36.
30. Herbert Waltzer, "In the Magic Lantern: Television Coverage of the 1964 National Conventions," *Public Opinion Quarterly*, Vol. 30 (Spring 1966), p. 37.

of the mixup, and it is unlikely to happen again. Nonetheless, some solid and simple improvements could be made to ensure that it will not recur. Suggestions made by the press that one person be given authority to deal with the news media and explain the ground rules of convention coverage to them well ahead of time doubtless would be seconded by all the media; but the party official assigned would have a thankless job.

The Democrats could well emulate the Republican arrangements procedures. The Republican arrangements panel is a large (fifty members or more) working committee that is closely coordinated with the activities of Josephine Good, who has been for more than a decade the national committee's executive director for the convention. The GOP arrangements committee has numerous subcommittees, including ones on periodicals and photographers, the press, and radio-television. The Democratic arrangements committee, in contrast, long was "largely a letterhead organization"[31] with fewer members, fewer meetings, and no subcommittees with specified jurisdictions. Nor have the Democrats had a professional convention manager. They have pleaded an inadequate budget for such a desirable luxury on a year-round basis; but in an election year at least the benefits surely outweigh the cost. For 1972 there will be a convention director and an arrangements committee of fifteen members, selected by the Democratic National Committee; one of their areas of responsibility will be communications and the news media. These officials could go far to plan better news coverage at the convention.

One major change in convention arrangements that is persistently recommended is the establishment of a permanent national convention center to be used by both parties every four years. Details of the proposals have varied; but some have suggested that it be financed by the television networks, which would save several million dollars each time they did not have to move their personnel

---

31. John F. Bibby and Herbert E. Alexander, *The Politics of National Convention Finances and Arrangements*, Study No. 14 (Princeton, N.J.: Citizens Research Foundation, no date), p. 24.

and equipment to two cities rather than a single site. An alternative way for the networks to encourage a single convention site would be for them to add their own financial incentives to a city's bids to the parties. Because of a fear of charges of undue interference in politics, the networks have been unwilling to support the convention center idea. The national parties too have been unenthusiastic; having all conventions in a single place would end the political flexibility and opportunity for choice that they now have in the site selection process.

ACCESS TO SOURCES

Generally, the exchange of information for publicity between politicians and the press has worked well except when the interests of politicians seeking privacy have clashed with the interests of reporters seeking news. Since 1952, television has gained access equal to that of the other media and has led the way in opening up more convention meetings to all the press. Indeed, some candidates and groups, like Lar Daly in his Uncle Sam costume seeking the presidency every four years, have been more eager for exposure in the news media than the media have been to report on their activities. Yet access remains a residual problem because political leaders always will need private meetings where they can speak their minds without fear of reprisal from anyone, including the opposition; while reporters, by the very nature of their trade, will want access to just those meetings because they are the most newsworthy.

At the 1968 Democratic convention, the problem of access for television took a new and undesirable turn when convention managers sought to play down demonstrations against the Vietnam war as bad publicity. Reporters viewed the demonstrations as more newsworthy than some of the more mundane convention events; the police, presumably under orders from the mayor, discouraged representatives of the news media from covering events in the streets. Television coverage of the demonstrations was inhibited by camera requirements. Convention officials refused on security grounds the networks' requests to permit cameras in the windows of the International Amphitheater and the Conrad Hilton Hotel, the major political headquarters located across the street from Grant Park, where the protesters assembled. The police would not allow mobile units from television networks to park in the streets. Meanwhile, although Chicago Mayor Richard Daley persuaded a local of the International Brotherhood of Electrical Workers to lift their ongoing strike at the Amphitheater, he did not get them to lift it at other important sites.[32] At the mercy of their equipment, the networks were able only with the greatest difficulty to cover the demonstrations, generally from the Hilton; and CBS technicians there have claimed that lighting cables were unplugged by Chicago policemen, who forcibly prevented them from turning the lights back on and thus from photographing the violent disorders outside the hotel.[33]

When such a conflict over access occurs, political leaders have the initial advantage because they can say no and make it stick. Yet the press has powers of reprisal; reporters can tell their audiences their own versions of what has happened, as they did about Chicago. Even though many viewers did not believe the television correspondents, the news coverage evidently harmed the Democratic cause. Perhaps more important, politicians believed that it did. The persistent loser in such a situation is the public, which is more confused and alienated than it is educated by what it learns or thinks it learns.

Especially in the clamor of a national convention, there is no sure or easy way to solve the problem of access to news sources. The solution requires restraint from reporters and politicians alike. While perhaps it is useless to recommend them, mutual understanding and cooperation between political leaders and the press are necessary to make the system work and to promote public

32. Whiteside, "Corridor of Mirrors," pp. 45–47.
33. *Ibid.*, pp. 49–50.

understanding.[34] Common courtesy and civilized discourse are equally desirable.

More specifically, rules governing the access of television cameras should be clarified. As was pointed out in Chapter 4, cameras and crews could be eliminated on nuisance grounds from the convention floor. Zoom lenses in cameras located on the periphery of the convention hall would enable television producers to get pictures to go with coverage by reporters. Meanwhile, the other media in pursuing their stories would be spared the annoyance of large amounts of electronic equipment, and confusion would be reduced for delegates and the public.

Cameras should not be prevented from covering legitimate news. The television networks' requests to place cameras outside the convention hall when events warrant seem on balance reasonable and desirable. As was evident at Chicago in 1968, television needs its cameras and equipment to get a story. Otherwise, it suffers in relation to the other news media. While the camera requests officially were denied at Chicago for security reasons, the denial obviously was intended to avoid public criticism of the convention and city leadership. But the public in this case clearly had a right to see what was going on. The officials' action suggested that they had something to hide. In the Langs' terms, the process of refraction resulted in an image of deception behind closed doors when viewers were told that television pictures were not permitted. Those in charge would have been served better if they permitted television cameras to cover what was obviously a major news story that was already being followed by the other media. There is no reason to believe that the party's candidates would have stood to lose more if television cameras had been permitted at the Chi-

34. Among the norms of interaction that have been suggested for more regularized relationships between politicans and the press by Delmer Dunn are the following: the press should not reveal the identity of its sources; the news media should remain scrupulously independent of politics; reporters should be told the truth; political leaders should not complain to a reporter's superiors; reporters should be treated fairly. Dunn, *Public Officials and the Press*, pp. 45–48.

cago demonstrations than they lost when cameras were forbidden and television people were harassed. Indeed, the candidates would have had an opportunity to show their ability to cope with the situation, as Eugene McCarthy did at the close of the convention and Edmund Muskie did during the course of the campaign. And the viewers would have had a better basis for making up their own minds.

CONTENT OF COVERAGE

At the conventions as elsewhere, the substance of news coverage is a perennial topic of debate because judgments concerning news are inherently matters of selectivity and hence are vulnerable to charges of bias. In political journalism, simply determining what is news may involve a decision of considerable consequence. Reporters choose which politicians to interview; thereby they offer to trade more publicity to some politicians than to others, not because they seek principally to foster the careers of certain politicians, but because they think they can get more news from them. Deciding how the story will be covered has additional political implications. The amount of coverage to be given to a particular story is a function of the extent of overall coverage, the arrangements for coverage, and access to news sources; it is also a matter of conscious choice by newsmen on professional grounds.

Television has special problems of news content, due partially to the nature of the medium—its powerful impact, the need for vast amounts of material, the sensitivity of an industry licensed by the government, and the controversiality of editorial decisions. Great concern among some political leaders about the actual or potential power of the television news producer at the conventions has given rise to the suggestion that when edited or spliced film is used in television news, this fact should be made known to the viewers. This would not limit the options of the producer; it would merely point out that some liberties had been taken with the taped visual report. The public would be offered a clearer understanding of what they were seeing. Yet virtually all television news film *is* edited because cameramen would rather get too much of a story than not enough. Hence the "edited film" label would be broadcast continually, if not continuously. There is a danger that through the process of refraction the viewers might receive thereby an image of manipulation by the television producers. Presumably most viewers are sophisticated enough to realize at least dimly that film editing is a necessary and honorable device not unlike editing newspaper copy, but the impact of such a device is doubtful.

The content of television coverage involves two interrelated dilemmas: the dilemma of length and that of fairness. As Kurt Lang has observed, the traditional pattern of "full and live coverage is not necessarily the most objective coverage."[35] The networks' vast investments in covering the conventions encourages a lengthy show that requires maximum exploitation of whatever stories can be found to fill the time. Not only may the frivolous or irrelevant get as much time as the significant; they may be made thereby to appear equally important. A 60-second interview with a movie star is balanced against a 60-second interview with a senator; giving them equal time implies that their views are equally weighty. Or, as Spiro Agnew summarized the values of the television producer: "One minute of Eldridge Cleaver is worth 10 minutes of Roy Wilkins."[36]

Access to important meetings, plus the reportorial ingenuity encouraged by the spending of vast amounts of time and money, also may lead to the screening of political events that are not spontaneous and unrehearsed. Thus, "although it's true that TV can really expose and reveal people . . . it's also frighteningly true that what is revealed can be controlled and arranged, and that the people out there who watch and defer to these revelations very rarely know the extent to which this is so."[37] Often politicians stage events for effect: a demonstration in front of television cameras, a strategi-

35. Testimony before the Commission on Rules of the Democratic National Committee (July 26, 1969), p. 7.

36. *Vital Speeches*, Vol. 36 (Dec. 1, 1969), p. 100.

37. Michael J. Arlen, "The Air: Moon Over Miami," *New Yorker*, Vol. 44 (Aug. 17, 1968), p. 82.

cally timed endorsement, a show of unity behind a state delegation chairman. But the media too can play the game. Theodore White has contended that television's intercutting of film of Chicago street demonstrations with the proceedings on the convention floor "created the most striking and false political picture of 1968—the nomination of a man for the American Presidency by the brutality and violence of merciless police."[38] Convinced that the Chicago authorities were preventing legitimate coverage of demonstrations near the 1968 Democratic convention, CBS ran a live interview with Mayor Daley, who blandly told the viewers that undue force was not being used in his city, juxtaposed with a film showing just the opposite—scores of police and National Guard troops with bayonets patrolling downtown streets.[39] The mayor was not informed, as he should have been under any reasonable standard of fairness, that the contradictory film was being used as he commented on the situation. While the CBS treatment did convey a general sense of what was going on in Chicago, the method did not allow Daley to react to, or even to be aware of, what constituted a filmed rebuttal to his statements.

Mayor Daley had the upper hand, however, in a similar drama— his interview with Walter Cronkite on the day after the CBS commentator had lashed into the management of the convention and related demonstrations. The mayor stated his case, saying that extreme security measures were necessary because of threats against the lives of political leaders and the people of Chicago. No one responded, not even to ask how much security was needed or how reliable the information about the threats was, or how all this necessitated security action against insurgent convention delegates inside the convention hall. Cronkite, who as a seasoned professional is rarely at a loss for words, evidently thought he had said enough already; no one else was present to discuss the fundamental problems with the mayor. The viewing public was left with two

38. Theodore H. White, *The Making of the President 1968* (Atheneum, 1969), p. 300.

39. See Whiteside, "Corridor of Mirrors," pp. 51–54.

sets of mutually contradictory statements and the image of a Cronkite–Daley handshake. Clearly both CBS and the Democratic party seemed unable to debate the issues seriously.

Some system is obviously needed that would allow all sides to speak, and preferably to respond to one another, thereby assuring the public a maximum opportunity to understand. This is not always easy to provide, particularly under the extremely trying conditions prevailing at Chicago in 1968. A better format would allow politicians to act as political leaders, honestly stating a case as they saw it, and reporters to follow up the issues in the best tradition of their profession. Discussions among several politicians with differing points of view would provide some perspective for the audience. If it were impossible to convene such a group, consecutive interviews by skilled reporters could serve a similar purpose.

Since the citizenry obtains nearly all its information about conventions from the news media, particularly television, the role of the media is clearly central to the democratic process. Given the frequently conflicting interests of politicians and reporters, firm and fair ground rules for news coverage are difficult to establish. Perhaps more than anything else a continuing effort is needed to provide new ways of educating the electorate (and a wider audience), not only with facts but also with varying perspectives on convention proceedings. The news media have done a good job since 1952 of making their audience more sophisticated about what goes on at conventions; what is needed now in addition is innovation and variety in interpretive reporting. This will require an effort on the part of politicians as well as journalists to help their audiences understand the significance of convention events—including discussions of new or possible changes in convention structure.

Chapter Seven

☆

SOLUTIONS

Who ever knew Truth put to the worse
in a free and open encounter?
John Milton

EACH OF THE MAJOR POLITICAL PARTIES has been seeking to benefit from a disastrous past convention rather than, in Santayana's phrase, being condemned to relive it. Fairness and democracy in presidential nominating procedures are the stated goals. This final chapter compares the merits of seeking to achieve those goals by restructuring national conventions with those of an alternative that long has had persistent advocates—a national presidential primary.

The Primary Alternative

Many thoughtful and articulate people, from Senate Majority Leader Mike Mansfield to the journalist Leonard Lurie,[1] have concluded that the presidential nominating convention is not viable. Emphasizing that it has been unfair, undemocratic, messy, and dull, they argue that in the era of an enlightened and expanding electorate the presidential convention will go the way of the horse and buggy—and that it should. Thus they have turned to a national primary as the only acceptable method for nominating presidential candidates.

1. Senator Mansfield has introduced numerous measures to establish a national presidential primary. For Lurie's views, see his *The King Makers* (Coward, McCann & Geoghegan, 1971), pp. 259–62.

A major problem in predicting the impact of a national presidential primary (or series of primaries held in all the states on the same day) is that there is no precedent by which to be guided. No other countries have the same kind of party system as the United States; none has a national primary. Statewide experience with presidential primaries is of dubious relevance. The best analysis that can be made is little more than informed speculation.

Advocates of a national primary contend that it is the most fair and democratic way of selecting candidates because it is based simply on the will of all the voters. Since the progressive era, supporters of this nominating procedure have argued further that candidates chosen in a primary would be more responsive to the voters and the public than are candidates who are named by political leaders in a convention or appointment system.

Others have been skeptical. They have contended variously that a national primary would produce an unrepresentative turnout at the polls, seriously weaken party organizations, and in the words of Nelson Polsby and Aaron Wildavsky, "restrict . . . presidential candidates to wealthy athletes."[2]

The available evidence shows that the turnout for state primaries has been smaller than it has for general elections and that those who did vote in those primaries sometimes differed significantly from the non-voters. The average turnout rate for all types of primaries has been just over 30 percent. For general elections, it has been well over 50 percent.[3] For the competitive presidential primaries (in the states where the outcome was in doubt), Austin Ranney has calculated that the mean turnout rate from 1948 to 1968 was 39 percent; for the presidential elections in the same years, the rate was 69 percent.[4] Moreover, presidential primary electorates—and primary electorates generally—have been un-

2. Nelson W. Polsby and Aaron B. Wildavsky, *Presidential Elections* (2nd ed.; Scribner's, 1968), p. 229.
3. Austin Ranney, "Turnout and Representation in Presidential Primary Elections," paper delivered at the annual meeting of the American Political Science Association, Chicago, Sept. 7–11, 1971, pp. 2–3.
4. *Ibid.*, p. 13.

representative of party adherents who did not vote.[5] Those who voted in primaries have been older and of higher income and occupational status than the non-voters. Ranney also found that voters in the 1968 presidential primaries in New Hampshire and Wisconsin differed significantly from non-voting party identifiers in their views on the issues—particularly in the intensity of their views. In addition Ranney noted that since not all the major presidential hopefuls were on the ballot, it was impossible to judge whether the primary results accurately reflected the candidate preferences of party voters.[6]

The problem of getting all the candidates on the ballot would be obviated in a national primary and could be remedied fairly readily by amending state laws in a series of state primaries; but some of the other problems of the representativeness of primaries are more intractable. Poorer people participate less than do more affluent people in virtually all political and organized social activities. And it is hardly surprising to learn that more people of all strata consider general elections to be important enough for them to cast a vote than are motivated to vote in primaries. Hence *party voters* in primaries may be very different from *party adherents* in the electorate. Probably more people would vote if there were a single national presidential primary or presidential primaries in all jurisdictions on a single day. But on the basis of what is known about voting behavior, it still seems likely that in most years fewer people would turn out for the primaries than for the general election and that voters as a group still would be of higher socioeconomic status than non-voters as a group. In this sense the delegates assembled at national conventions can be more representative than are party voters in a primary of the demographic characteristics and conceivably even of the candidate preferences of all rank-and-file partisans.

Many political scientists have concluded further that primary elections tend to destroy party organization. V. O. Key, Jr. stud-

5. *Ibid.*, p. 6.
6. *Ibid.*, pp. 11–12.

ied nominations of candidates for state legislatures in two-party states over time and found that at that level the primary effectively transferred the election decision to the majority-party primary and caused the minority party to atrophy. This, in turn, undermined the two-party system as the minority party became less important than the factions in the majority party.[7] Moreover, as Polsby and Wildavsky have pointed out, shifting the real decision to the majority party primary provides an opportunity for a greater number of candidates, some of whom perhaps are unqualified or demagogic, to make a better showing than they would have made in a two-party race. Polsby and Wildavsky add that such a situation is confusing to many voters, for whom the party endorsement has been the principal basis of decision in two-party contests.[8]

Yet the evidence on the effects of primaries is difficult to interpret. V. O. Key specifically cautioned that his findings might not apply to primary elections in larger jurisdictions. There are probably fewer weak minority parties at the state level in the 1970s than there were during the 1950s, when Key published his article. Party organizations are not necessarily weak in states that have primaries. Party leaders may lend their efforts to structuring the primaries by endorsing candidates or running slates so that they have some measure of control over the outcome. Nor are party organizations always strong in convention states. The most likely effect a national primary would have on party organization is that a closer link would be forged between national candidate organizations and their state and local affiliates.

Much has been made of the financial and physical strain that candidates would have to endure if a national presidential primary were adopted. Already the costs have been enormous. The assumption has been that if the primary system were extended from twenty-three jurisdictions to fifty states plus the District of Columbia and perhaps the territories, the amount of television adver-

7. V. O. Key, Jr., "The Direct Primary and Party Structure," *American Political Science Review*, Vol. 48 (March 1954), pp. 1–26.
8. *Presidential Elections*, pp. 229–31.

tising, handshaking, staff work, public speaking, and all the other trappings of recent presidential campaigns would increase by a corresponding amount. Perhaps it would; and perhaps not. The outer limits of human endurance, elaborate campaigns, and financial outlays may be approaching. Furthermore, even the existence of those outer limits might mean that primary nominating campaigns would emphasize television more and active personal campaigning by candidates less. Television costs are more easily traced and regulated than are most other kinds of campaign expenses.[9] In any case, the problem of money would have to be dealt with in any proposal for a national presidential primary.

Many more technical issues also would have to be resolved in establishing a national primary or a nationwide system of state primaries. Presumably, national voter qualification requirements and some system for putting candidates on the ballot would be needed. There has been a continuing debate among political scientists about the fairest rules for a model primary law. Most prefer a primary that is closed to voters who are not party registrants; others argue that little if any "raiding" by the opposition goes on in open primaries. In addition, there is the vital question whether there would be a single plurality primary—in which case the winner might well have substantially less than 50 percent of the vote—or an initial primary plus a runoff if no one obtained a simple majority—in which instance the candidate who had the most votes initially might lose the runoff.

The fundamental question about a national primary is its capacity to choose the candidate most favored by party voters. When there is a clear front-runner, the primary (like a convention) easily produces a winner. When there are only two candidates, one automatically has a majority. But when the field is larger, difficult problems of social choice arise in either a convention or a primary. Essentially, a primary is a means of measuring attitude distributions—and not a method of arriving at agreement. There can be no

9. See Delmer D. Dunn, *Financing Presidential Campaigns* (Brookings Institution, 1972).

assurance that either a candidate who finished first in a single primary or one who triumphed in a runoff contest would be the preference of most party voters.[10]

Toward Fair and Democratic Conventions

The restructured convention appears to be the better choice. A national primary has inherent limitations and uncertainties. Unlike the primary, the model convention described in this book always would produce a party nominee who was the choice of a majority of the party voters' representatives, who in turn would have been selected on the basis of their candidate preferences. If fairness and democracy can be assured at the convention, as has been suggested here, there will be no need to change to a national primary system—which has not always provided the ultimate in those qualities where it has been used.

In the first chapter of this book, the convention problem was posed as what the nature of the institution for nominating presidential candidates should be, and particularly how the new demand for fairness and democracy could be reconciled with the traditional aims of efficiency, legitimacy, reasonableness, and party consensus. The short answer that emerges from this analysis is that the convention should be a representative and sometimes deliberative body, of which both party activists and the party-in-the-electorate are vital organs.

Specifically, conventions should operate as follows:

1. The convention should be representative of the party's presidential constituency—both those who have voted for its past nominees and those who might vote for its future candidates. In terms of apportionment, this principle means that each state's votes

10. Studies by Paul T. David suggest that whereas divided conventions more often select nominees from the ideological center, primaries may more often select from the extremes of the party. See "Experimental Approaches to Vote-counting Theory in Nominating Choice," *American Political Science Review*, Vol. 56 (September 1962), pp. 673–76.

should be allocated partially on the basis of its past presidential voting record and partially according to its population. The exact ratio of the two factors in the formula might vary somewhat; the simplest solution would be to apportion half the votes on the basis of party voting and half for population. Convention committees and the body that acts for the convention between its quadrennial meetings should be apportioned on the same bases as the full assembly.

2. The delegates should reflect accurately the candidate preferences of their rank-and-file constituencies. Hence they should be chosen on that basis, either in a party primary or in state and local conventions that are apportioned according to the above rules and that consist of participants who themselves have been elected by the party voters for this particular purpose. Racial, sexual, age, and income groups should be represented in the delegations in proportion to their share of the party's presidential constituency. Procedures for awarding credentials should be widely known, administered equally to all, and not systematically biased for or against any of the party's factions. To these ends, national standards of delegate selection should require wide public participation, demographic representation, and party loyalty by the delegates. Reconciling public participation and demographic representation will not be easy in practice, but the parties must find ways to do it.

3. The convention must be able to carry on its activities efficiently. This objective would be enhanced by smaller conventions with no more than 1,500 delegates, fewer alternates, fewer other people in the hall, and smaller committees. In addition, parliamentary rules should be adopted and enforced that would balance the values of efficiency and of giving each participant the opportunity for rational, deliberative judgment. In other words, ordinary delegates should have time to read committee reports before voting; and any substantial opposition (5 or 10 percent of the committee) should have an opportunity to present a minority report to be voted up or down by the convention. Delegates seeking recogni-

tion ordinarily should arrange their motions with the chairman in advance; unless their requests are frivolous, they should be granted. Petition requirements and the rules for allocating speech time should discourage minor candidacies. For nominating and voting purposes, the names of the states should be called in an order determined by lot. Procedures such as the old unit rule, which inhibited delegates from voting as they wished, should be prohibited. Any delegate should be able to obtain a poll of his or her delegation; roll call votes should be required at the demand of a substantial fraction—20 or 25 percent—of the delegates.

4. Only a relatively few people have the interest, competence, and breadth of understanding required to write a party platform. It is essential in such an undertaking that all partisans have the opportunity to express their views at platform hearings, that a full range of party documents be assayed in the deliberations, that the presidential candidates be represented in the writing of the platform, that the platform committee be apportioned according to each state's share of the party's presidential constituency, that the delegates have at least one day to study the draft before voting on it, that a copy of the statement approved by the convention be made available to anyone who wants it, and that the victorious party continue to use the platform as the basis for its policies and programs in governing.

5. Fairness also is needed in coverage of the convention by the news media, which link the candidates and party activists with the party-in-the-electorate and the public. The most important medium is television—the source of most public information about politics. All the media should have equal access to legitimate news stories and adequate facilities for doing their jobs. For their part, the journalists should experiment with different formats for presenting news about conventions and various perspectives for interpreting convention events. Commentators should do much more to elucidate the serious issues that are discussed at conventions. A high level of public understanding of convention events is necessary if the institution is to be a viable aspect of democratic politics.

Solving the Convention Problem

What is needed at conventions is what the founding fathers of the republic sought as they drafted the United States Constitution—formally written, known, and essentially permanent rules designed to control dangerous excesses threatened by the clash of human wills in politics. Written constitutions alone cannot insure fairness and democracy, which require political leaders who will abide by the spirit of those values; but rules that state such objectives are also necessary because, in James Madison's words, "enlightened statesmen will not always be at the helm."[11]

The changes in the convention system proposed here should serve to demonstrate the capacity of a mechanism based on the intense pursuit of many particular interests to contribute to norms of a wider public interest. The effort to open conventions to public scrutiny is not absurdly idealistic in the face of the innate selfishness of human nature. On the contrary. Either the major institutions of the United States must operate to fulfill the values that they were founded to serve, or they risk perishing in a tide of public disgust. Thus, in large measure, the convention problem symbolizes the problem of politics in a democracy during the final third of the twentieth century.

11. Jacob E. Cooke (ed.), *The Federalist*, Paper No. 10 (Wesleyan University Press, 1961), p. 60.

CONFERENCE PARTICIPANTS

JOHN F. BIBBY *University of Wisconsin—Milwaukee*

KENNETH A. BODE *Center for Political Reform*

WILLIAM J. CROTTY *Northwestern University*

ANDREW J. GLASS *National Journal*

JOHN H. KESSEL *Ohio State University*

DONALD R. MATTHEWS *Brookings Institution*

DANIEL A. MAZMANIAN *Brookings Institution*

FRANK MUNGER *University of North Carolina*

JUDITH H. PARRIS *Brookings Institution*

GILBERT Y. STEINER *Brookings Institution (Chairman)*

JAMES L. SUNDQUIST *Brookings Institution*

SIDNEY WISE *Franklin & Marshall College*

SELECTED BIBLIOGRAPHY

THIS BIBLIOGRAPHY is not intended as a complete list of everything written on conventions nor as a catalogue of every point of view about the subject. A complete bibliography would require another book. And most of the written opinions about current issues have come from those upon whom the burden of proof lies—the proponents of various changes in the convention system.

Instead, this bibliography aims at guiding the interested reader to sources for further study. It includes both the most authoritative and the most provocative published books and articles about conventions. Additional works used directly in the preparation of this book are cited in the footnotes.

Most of the publications listed may be found in any large library or obtained through its inter-library loan facilities. Reports issued by the Republican and Democratic national committees are available to the public without cost so long as the supply lasts. The former is located at 310 First Street, S.E., Washington, D.C. 20003. The Democratic National Committee's address is 2600 Virginia Avenue, N.W., Washington, D.C. 20037.

General

Burns, James MacGregor. "The Case for the Smoke-Filled Room," *New York Times Magazine*, June 15, 1952.

Carleton, William G. "How Free Are the Nominating Conventions?" *Virginia Quarterly Review*, Vol. 40 (Spring 1964).

———. "The Revolution in the Presidential Nominating Convention," *Political Science Quarterly*, Vol. 72 (June 1957).

David, Paul T., Ralph M. Goldman, and Richard C. Bain. *The Politics of National Party Conventions*. Washington: Brookings Institution, 1960.

Davis, James W. *Springboard to the White House: Presidential Primaries:*

How They Are Fought and Won. New York: Thomas Y. Crowell, 1967.

Polsby, Nelson W. "Decisionmaking at the National Conventions," *Western Political Quarterly*, Vol. 13 (September 1960).

————, and Aaron B. Wildavsky. *Presidential Elections: Strategies of American Electoral Politics.* 3rd ed. New York: Scribner's, 1971.

The Current Debate

Brightman, Samuel C. "The Democrats Open the Door," *Nation*, Vol. 212 (May 3, 1971).

Glass, Andrew J., and Jonathan Cottin. "Democratic Reform Drive Falters as Spotlight Shifts to Presidential Race," *National Journal*, Vol. 3 (June 19, 1971).

Historical

Bain, Richard C. *Convention Decisions and Voting Records.* Washington: Brookings Institution, 1960.

Bryan, William Jennings. *A Tale of Two Conventions.* New York: Funk & Wagnalls, 1912.

Chester, Lewis, Godfrey Hodgson, and Bruce Page. *An American Melodrama: The Presidential Campaign of 1968.* New York: Viking Press, 1969.

Congressional Quarterly Service. *The Presidential Nominating Conventions—1968.* Washington: Congressional Quarterly Service, 1968.

David, Paul T., Malcolm Moos, and Ralph M. Goldman. *Presidential Nominating Politics in 1952.* 5 vols. Baltimore: Johns Hopkins Press, 1954.

Eaton, Herbert. *Presidential Timber: A History of Nominating Conventions, 1868–1960.* New York: Free Press, 1964.

Halstad, Murat. *Caucuses of 1860: A History of the National Political Conventions of the Current Presidential Campaign.* Columbus, Ohio: Follett, Foster & Company, 1860.

Hyman, Herbert H., and Paul B. Sheatsley. "The Political Appeal of President Eisenhower," *Public Opinion Quarterly*, Vol. 17 (Winter 1953–54).

Kessel, John H. *The Goldwater Coalition: Republican Strategies in 1964.* Indianapolis: Bobbs-Merrill, 1968.

Lurie, Leonard. *The King Makers.* New York: Coward, McCann & Geoghegan, 1971.

McCarthy, Eugene J. *The Year of the People.* New York: Doubleday, 1969.

Thomson, Charles A. H., and Frances M. Shattuck. *The 1956 Presidential Campaign.* Washington: Brookings Institution, 1960.

Tillett, Paul, ed. *Inside Politics: The National Conventions, 1960.* America's Politics Series. Dobbs Ferry, N.Y.: Oceana Publications, 1962.

———. "The National Conventions," in Milton C. Cummings, Jr., ed., *The National Election of 1964.* Washington: Brookings Institution, 1966.

———. "The National Conventions," in Paul T. David, ed., *The Presidential Election and Transition 1960–1961.* Washington: Brookings Institution, 1961.

White, F. Clifton, with William J. Gill. *Suite 3505: The Story of the Draft Goldwater Movement.* New Rochelle, N.Y.: Arlington House, 1967.

White, Theodore H. *The Making of the President 1960.* New York: Atheneum, 1961.

———. *The Making of the President 1964.* New York: Atheneum, 1965.

———. *The Making of the President 1968.* New York: Atheneum, 1969.

Apportionment and Size

Bellamy, Calvin. "Applicability of the Fourteenth Amendment to the Allocation of Delegates to the Democratic National Convention," *George Washington Law Review,* Vol. 38 (July 1970).

Chicago Home Rule Commission. *Chicago's Government: Its Structural Modernization and Home Rule Problems.* Chicago: University of Chicago Press, 1954.

deGrazia, Alfred. *Essay on Apportionment and Representative Government.* Washington: American Enterprise Institute for Public Policy Research, 1963.

Dixon, Robert G., Jr. *Democratic Representation: Reapportionment in Law and Politics.* New York: Oxford University Press, 1968.

Pennock, J. Roland, and John W. Chapman, eds. *Representation.* (Nomos 10.) New York: Atherton Press, 1968.

Pitkin, Hanna F. *The Concept of Representation.* Berkeley: University of California Press, 1967.

Sayre, Wallace S., and Judith H. Parris. *Voting for President: The Electoral College and the American Political System.* Washington: Brookings Institution, 1970.

Delegate Selection and Credentials

"Constitutional Safeguards in the Selection of Delegates to Presidential Nominating Conventions," *Yale Law Journal*, Vol. 78 (June 1969).

Democratic National Committee. Commission on Party Structure and Delegate Selection. *Mandate for Reform*. Washington: Democratic National Committee, 1970.

Holtzman, Abraham. "The Loyalty Pledge Controversy in the Democratic Party," in Paul Tillett, ed., *Cases on Party Organization*. New York: McGraw-Hill, 1963.

Niemi, Richard G., and M. Kent Jennings. "Intraparty Communications and the Selection of Delegates to a National Convention," *Western Political Quarterly*, Vol. 22 (March 1969).

Republican National Committee. Delegates and Organizations Committee. *Progress Report*. 2 parts. Washington: Republican National Committee, 1971.

Schmidt, John R., and Wayne W. Whalen. "Credentials Contests at the 1968—and 1972—Democratic National Conventions," *Harvard Law Review*, Vol. 82 (May 1969).

Segal, Eli. "Delegate Selection Standards: The Democratic Party's Experience," *George Washington Law Review*, Vol. 38 (July 1970).

U.S. Congress. Senate. Library. *Nomination and Election of the President and Vice President of the United States Including the Manner of Selecting Delegates to National Political Conventions*. Published each presidential election year. Washington: Government Printing Office.

Delegates and Delegations

Bunzel, John H., and Eugene C. Lee. "The California Democratic Delegation of 1960," in Edwin A. Bock and Alan K. Campbell, eds., *Case Studies in American Government*. Englewood Cliffs, N.J.: Prentice-Hall, 1962.

Marvick, Dwaine, and Samuel J. Eldersveld. "National Convention Leadership: 1952 and 1956," *Western Political Quarterly*, Vol. 14 (March 1961).

Munger, Frank, and James Blackhurst. "Factionalism in the National Conventions, 1940–1964: An Analysis of Ideological Consistency in State Delegation Voting," *Journal of Politics*, Vol. 27 (May 1965).

Pomper, Gerald M. "Factionalism in the 1968 National Conventions: An Extension of Research Findings," *Journal of Politics*, Vol. 33 (August 1971).

Soule, John W., and James W. Clarke. "Amateurs and Professionals: A Study of Delegates to the 1968 Democratic National Convention," *American Political Science Review*, Vol. 64 (September 1970).

—— and ——. "Issue Conflict and Consensus: A Comparative Study of Democratic and Republican Delegates to the 1968 National Conventions," *Journal of Politics*, Vol. 33 (February 1971).

Rules and Arrangements

Bibby, John F., and Herbert E. Alexander. *The Politics of National Convention Finances and Arrangements*. Study No. 14. Princeton: Citizens' Research Foundation, no date.

Cotter, Cornelius P., and Bernard C. Hennessy. *Politics Without Power: The National Party Committees*. Chicago: Atherton Press, 1964.

Democratic National Committee. Commission on Rules. "Determinations of the Commission on Rules With Respect to the National Nominating Convention." Processed. Washington: Democratic National Committee, 1971. Reprinted in *Congressional Record*, daily ed., Oct. 21, 1971, pp. E11182–87.

Republican National Committee. *Rules Adopted by the Republican National Convention Held at Miami Beach, Florida, August 5, 1968*. Washington: Republican National Committee, no date.

Platform

Cooke, Edward F. "Drafting the 1952 Platforms," *Western Political Quarterly*, Vol. 9 (September 1956).

David, Paul T. "Party Platforms as National Plans," *Public Administration Review*, Vol. 31 (May–June 1971).

Pomper, Gerald M. "Controls and Influence in American Elections (Even 1968)," *American Behavioral Scientist*, Vol. 13 (November–December 1969).

——. *Elections in America: Control and Influence in Democratic Politics*. New York: Dodd, Mead & Company, 1970.

Ranney, Austin. *The Doctrine of Responsible Party Government: Its Origins and Present State*. Urbana: University of Illinois Press, 1954.

Shattschneider, E. E. *Party Government*. American Government in Action Series. New York: Holt, Rinehart & Winston, 1942.

Sundquist, James L. *Politics and Policy: The Eisenhower, Kennedy, and Johnson Years*. Washington: Brookings Institution, 1968.

News Media

Bogart, Leo. *The Age of Television.* 2nd ed. New York: Frederick Ungar, 1958.

Efron, Edith. *The News Twisters.* Los Angeles: Nash Publishing, 1971.

Erskine, Hazel. "The Polls: Opinion of the News Media," *Public Opinion Quarterly,* Vol. 34 (Winter 1970–1971).

Lang, Kurt, and Gladys Engel Lang. *Politics and Television.* Chicago: Quadrangle Books, 1968.

McDowell, Charles, Jr. "Carnival of Excess: TV at the Conventions," *Atlantic,* Vol. 222 (July 1968).

Robinson, John P. "Public Reaction to Political Protest: Chicago 1968," *Public Opinion Quarterly,* Vol. 34 (Spring 1970).

Thomson, Charles A. H. *Television and Presidential Politics: The Experience in 1952 and the Problems Ahead.* Washington: Brookings Institution, 1956.

Waltzer, Herbert. "In the Magic Lantern: Television Coverage of the 1964 National Conventions," *Public Opinion Quarterly,* Vol. 30 (Spring 1966).

Whale, John. *The Half-Shut Eye: Television and Politics in Britain and America.* New York: Macmillan, 1969; London: St. Martin's Press, 1969.

Whiteside, Thomas. "Corridor of Mirrors: The Television Editorial Process, Chicago," *Columbia Journalism Review* (Winter 1968/1969).

INDEX

Adams, Sherman, 117
Agar, Herbert, 106
Agnew, Spiro T., 38, 43; on news media, 95, 144, 148, 169
Alabama, 23, 29n, 43
Alaska, 29, 38
Albert, Carl, 2, 125
Alexander, Herbert E., 164n
Alternates, 87; Democratic reforms, 89, 92–93; floor access of, 94–95; Republican reforms, 88–89
American Broadcasting Company, 159–63
Americans for Democratic Action, 19
Appointment system: in delegate selection, 52–54, 58, 71, 73
Apportionment system: alternative plans, 36–50; bonus votes, 20, 22–23, 26–27, 29, 34, 40–41, 49; comparisons, 42–50; Democratic, 18–20, 27–36, 47–48, 50, 87; formulas for, 16–17; large vs. small states, 41, 48; lawsuits, 18–21; mixed proposal, 42–43, 45, 47–50; party official proposal, 36–38; by party voting, 17–18, 40–42, 178; by population, 17–18, 38–40, 178; Republican, 17–28, 34–35, 43, 45, 47, 50. *See also* Delegate selection
Arlen, Michael J., 169n
Associated Press (AP), 158
Atlantic City, 117

Baar, Carl, 36–37
Bagehot, Walter, 115
Bailey, Stephen K., 152n
Bain, Richard C., 1n, 18n, 42n, 62n, 114n
Barkley, Alben, 29
Bayh, Birch, 57
Behavior at conventions, 4–6; Democratic National Convention *1968*, 106–7, 165–68, 170–71; Eisenhower on,

7–8, 11, 154; reform proposals, 107–8; Republican reforms, 11–12
Bell & Howell Company, 119
Berelson, Bernard, 142
Bibby, John F., 164n
Blacks. *See* Minorities
Bliss, Ray C., 121
Bode, Kenneth A., 19, 54n
Boggs, Hale, 125
Bolton, Arthur K., 19
Bond, Julian, 54
Bonus votes, 40–41, 49; in Democratic apportionment formulas, 29, 34; and Georgia suit, 20; origin, 27; in Republican apportionment formula, 22–23, 26. *See also* Party voting
Bowles, Chester, 123, 125–26, 129
Branigan, Roger E., 58n
Brewster, Daniel B., 58n
Brinkley, David, 147
Broder, David S., 156n
Bryan, William Jennings, 17
Bryce, James, 13
Bush, Prescott S., 117, 125
Butler, Paul M., 125, 129
Byrd, Harry F., 30n

California, 19, 43, 55–56
Canada: apportionment formula, 36–38; platform reform, 132
Canal Zone: apportionment system, 29; delegation size, 88
Candidates. *See* Presidential candidates
Carlino, Joseph F., 127
Center for Political Reform, 19
Chancellor, John, 151, 154
"Checkers" speech, 144
Chester, Lewis, 119n
Chicago, 2, 10, 82, 144–45, 148–50, 165–68, 170–71
Chisholm, Shirley, 71

Civil rights: Democratic platforms, 118, 121, 123–24, 126, 155; Republican platforms, 117, 120. *See also* Minorities

Clarke, James W., 4*n*, 59, 85*n*

Cleaver, Eldridge, 169

Colorado, 125

Columbia Broadcasting System (CBS), 59, 144, 154, 163, 166, 170–71

Commission on Party Structure and Delegate Selection (Democratic), 10, 19, 51, 68; on delegate selection, 69–71; minority group proposal, 75

Commission on Rules (Democratic), 10, 19, 30, 69, 73; on apportionment, 49–50; on committees, 90, 99–100; on convention size, 92–93; and credentials process, 68; on floor access, 94; on floor debate, 101; on news media, 96; on platform, 130–32, 136, 140; on procedural rules, 98; on voting, 105

Committee on Convention Reforms (Republican), 12

Committees (national convention): delegate selection, 90; minority reports, 100–101; reforms, 99–100, 178; size of, 89–91. *See also* Platform

Congressional caucus, 1

Congressional districts: in apportionment formulas, 17, 21–22

Congressman: in apportionment formulas, 21–23, 29, 34

Connecticut, 125

Conservative party (Canada), 36

Convention system: in delegate selection, 52–55, 73, 84

Cooke, Edward F., 118*n*

Cooke, Jacob E., 86*n*, 180*n*

Coordinating Committee (Republican), 129

Cottin, Jonathan, 57*n*

Credentials Committee (Democratic), 100

Credentials Committee (Republican), 11

Credentials contests: in delegate selection, 62–68

Critical Issues Council (Republican), 129

Cronin, Thomas E., 3*n*

Cronkite, Walter, 152, 170–71

Crotty, William J., 87*n*

Daley, Richard, 82*n*, 166, 170–71

Daly, Lar, 165

Dauer, Manning J., 58*n*

David, Paul T., 1*n*, 11*n*, 18*n*, 42*n*, 62*n*, 89–90, 113, 114*n*, 119*n*, 143*n*, 177*n*

Delaware, 43

Delegate selection, 3; alternative standards, 68–80; appointment system, 52–54, 58, 71, 73; by convention, 52–55, 73, 84; credentials contests, 9, 62–68; Democratic reforms, 69–71, 73, 75, 84, 91–92; demographic question, 12, 74–77, 178; institutions for, 52–58; judicial regulation, 78–80; loyalty requirements, 77–78, 178; by primary system, 14, 52–53, 55–58, 73; reform effect, 84–85; Republican reforms, 11–12, 69, 71–75, 92. *See also* Apportionment system; Delegates

Delegates: alternates, 88–89, 92–95, 178; characteristics of, 58–62; income level, 59; mandate-independence issue, 14, 85–86; reform effect, 84–85

Delegates and Organizations (DO) Committee (Republican), 130; *1972* guidelines, 71–73; on delegate selection, 74–75; minority recommendations, 12, 69, 90–91; nomination reforms, 102; on procedural rules, 99; roll call reform, 103; voting proposals, 105

Democratic Advisory Council, 110, 128

Democratic National Committee, 94; alternate rules, 93; and apportionment system, 18–19, 28–30, 50, 87; convention arrangements, 164; convention voting rights, 37; credentials contest, 65, 67; Georgia suit, 20; platform role, 118; procedural rules, 98

Democratic National Convention: *1860*, 94; *1924*, 151; *1948*, 110; *1956*, 126; *1960*, 94, 125–26; *1964*, 65–67, 87, 117, 149, 155; *1968*, 87, 110; behavior, 2, 106–7, 165–68, 170–71; credentials contest, 67–68; delegate characteristics, 59–60; delegate selection, 9; factions in, 2, 54, 149–50; and news media, 95, 142, 144–45, 148–51, 163–67, 170–71; platform of, 118–19, 126–27; security in, 93–94; unit rule ban in, 104–5; *1972*, 104–5, 164

Democratic party: alternate reforms, 93; apportionment system, 18–20, 27–36, 46–48, 50; credentials contest, 64–68; delegate selection system, 69–71, 73, 75, 84, 91–92; factions in, 27–28, 35–36; Georgia suit, 20; minority groups in, 70; political style, 11; procedural rules of, 98–106

Democratic Policy Council, 129

Demonstrations, 101–2

Derge, David R., 58*n*
Dewey, Thomas E., 26
Direct primary, 7
Dirksen, Everett M., 122, 125
Discrimination. *See* Civil rights; Minorities
District of Columbia, 19–20, 175; delegate selection, 53; delegation size, 88; Democratic apportionment for, 29–31; Republican apportionment for, 22–23
DO Committee. *See* Delegates and Organizations Committee
Dulles, John Foster, 117
Dunn, Delmer D., 153*n*, 156*n*, 167*n*, 176*n*
Dunne, Finley Peter, 16

Eaton, Herbert, 18*n*, 63*n*
Eisenhower, Dwight D., 6, 7*n*, 34, 97, 117, 120, 124, 129, 155; on convention behavior, 7–8, 11, 154; credentials contest *1952*, 62–64; and South, 26; television use, 152
Electoral college: in apportionment formulas, 18, 21, 29–30, 38–40, 45, 47–48, 50. *See also* Population
English, John F., 42
Erskine, Hazel, 145*n*
Ethnic groups. *See* Minorities
Ex officio delegates, 37, 70, 72
Expenditures: in delegate selection, 69–71, 75; in direct primary, 7; in national primary proposal, 175—76; in primary system, 56–57

Fair play amendment, 63–64, 97, 149
Favorite son candidates, 56, 58
Fourteenth Amendment, 79
Fractional voting, 91
Frankfurter, Felix, 79
Fraser, Donald M., 10
Freedom Democratic party, 65–67, 149
Froman, Lewis A., Jr., 81

Gallup poll, 145
Georgia, 19–20, 54, 64, 67, 118
Gill, William J., 107*n*
Ginn, Rosemary, 12
Glass, Andrew J., 57*n*
Goldman, Ralph M., 1*n*, 11*n*, 18*n*, 42*n*, 62*n*, 114*n*
Goldwater, Barry M., 64, 120, 124–25, 129, 135, 142, 155
Good, Josephine, 164
Governor: in delegate selection, 53–54; in Democratic apportionment formula,
29, 34; in Republican apportionment formula, 21, 23
Grant Park, 166
Gray v. Sanders (1963), 20*n*
Great Britain, 1
Guam, 22, 88

Hahn, Harlan, 89*n*
Hall, Leonard, 121
Hamer, Fannie Lou, 65–67
Harriman, Averell, 124
Harris, Fred R., 10
Hatfield, Mark, 152
Hawaii, 29
Henry, Aaron E., 67
Hess, Stephen, 109*n*
Hickey, Neil, 157*n*
Hodgson, Godfrey, 119*n*
Hoover, Herbert, 117
Hughes, Harold E., 9
Humphrey, Hubert H., 38, 43, 47–48, 53, 61, 82*n*, 119, 124, 148, 154

Income level, of delegates, 59
International Brotherhood of Electrical Workers, 166

Jackson, Andrew, 1, 28
Johnson, Loch K., 89*n*
Johnson, Lyndon B., 30, 58*n*, 132, 135; *1964* election, 31, 87; *1968* platform, 117, 124; and Freedom Democratic party, 66–67

Kefauver, Estes, 124
Kennedy, Edward M., 151
Kennedy, John F., 30, 34, 123, 126, 134, 152
Kennedy-Nixon debates, 143
Kennedy, Robert F., 58*n*, 123
Kessel, John H., 119*n*, 120, 121*n*, 124*n*
Key, V. O., Jr., 174–75
King, Edward, 67

Laird, Melvin R., 121–22, 125, 129
Lamb, Karl A., 119*n*, 121, 127
Lane, Robert E., 61*n*
Lang, Gladys, 107*n*, 146–47, 167
Lang, Kurt, 146–47, 167, 169
Lasswell, Harold D., 16*n*, 112*n*
Leadership, party, 175; in delegate selection, 52–58; in national convention, 82–84. *See also* Democratic National Committee; Republican National Committee; State chairman

Liberal party (Canada), 36, 132
Lincoln, Abraham, 94
Lindsay, John, 71
Lipset, Seymour Martin, 6n
Literacy tests, 75
Lodge, Henry Cabot, 152
Louisiana, 29, 64, 125
Loyal Democrats of Mississippi, 67
Loyalty requirement, in delegate selection, 77–78
Lurie, Leonard, 172
Lyle, Jack, 143n

Macy, Henry, 58n
Maddox, Lester G., 20, 54
Madison, James, 86, 180
Mansfield, Mike, 172
Martin, Ralph G., 11n
MacArthur, Douglas, 146–47
McCarthy, Eugene, 6, 9, 53, 82n, 92, 123, 143, 152, 168
McCormack, John W., 118, 125
McCormick, Anne O'Hare, 11
McDowell, Charles, Jr., 155n, 163n
McGovern, George S., 10, 71
McGovern-Fraser Commission. See Commission on Rules
Media. See News media
Mencken, H. L., 6
Miller, Arthur, 82n
Millikin, Eugene, 125
Milton, John, 172
Minorities: committee delegates, 74–75, 90–91; in credentials contest, 65–67; in delegate selection, 12, 58–62, 69–72, 74–77; reformist debate, 37–38, 178; roll call reform, 105. See also Civil rights; Women
Minority candidates. See Presidential candidates
Minority reports, 100–101, 118–19, 131, 178
Mississippi, 118; in apportionment system, 23, 26, 29; in credentials contest, 65–67; Freedom Democratic party, 65–67, 149
Moos, Malcolm, 1n, 11n, 109n, 152n
Muskie, Edmund S., 38, 43, 168

Namenwirth, J. Zvi, 112n
National Broadcasting Company (NBC), 147, 151, 154, 163
National chairman, 5, 124–25
National committee proposal, 135–37

National convention: alternates, 92–95; behavior in, 4–8, 11, 18, 106–8, 154, 165–68, 170–71; chairman, 5, 124–25; committees, 89–91, 99–101, 178; characteristics of, 3–6, 81–86; definition of, 2, 16–17; evaluation, 6–8, 12–15; floor access, 12, 93–96; leadership, 5, 82–84; length of, 4, 8, 12; midterm proposal, 137–39; minority candidates, 8, 71, 83–84, 97; minority reports, 100–101, 131, 178; national primary alternative, 172–77; news media in, 95–96, 149–53, 159–65, 168–71; nominations, 101–3; procedural rules, 96–106; reform of, 3, 12, 84–85, 117–80; roll call, 102–3, 105; sites, 149–50, 164–65; size of, 86–96, 106, 178; staff, 5–6, 86, 97, 162–64; state chairman role, 55, 82–84, 92, 140; television, 14, 143–44, 149–52, 156–57; voting reform proposal, 105–6. See also Apportionment system; Delegate selection; Platform
National Farmers' Union, 76
National Guard, 170
New England, 43, 45, 48
New Hampshire, 94, 174
New Mobilization Committee to End the War in Vietnam, 154
New York, 19, 38, 43, 89
News media, 4, 6, 8, 12; bias charges, 14, 144–45, 147–48; content, 168–71; convention arrangements for, 88, 95–96, 162–65; and convention site, 149–50, 164–65; and credentials contests, 74; in delegate selection process, 74; in Democratic National Convention *1968*, 95, 142, 144–45, 148–51, 163–67, 170–71; effect on convention, 149–53, 158–62, 179; and political leaders, 153–58, 165–68; printed, 158; public influence, 143–49; radio, 157–58; reform proposal, 179; Republican National Convention *1964*, 142, 154; television, 143–44, 149–52, 156–57
Nielsen ratings, 143, 161
Nixon, Richard M., 51, 119n, 155; *1960* race, 26, 125, 152; *1968* election, 12, 23, 38, 43, 61, 130, 148; "Checkers" speech, 144; Kennedy debates, 143; Rockefeller compact, 120–22, 126

Ogden, Daniel M., Jr., 119n
O'Hara, James G., 10, 30, 49, 90

O'Hara Commission on Rules. *See* Commission on Rules
Oklahoma, 53, 125
Ostrogorski, M., 6

Page, Bruce, 119n
Party committees, 52–54
Party platform. *See* Platform
Party voting: in apportionment formulas, 17, 19, 21–23, 26, 29–34, 40–42, 45, 47, 49, 178; in delegate selection, 70. *See also* Bonus votes
Peace movement, 155
Percy, Charles H., 119, 121, 125
Permanent organization committee, 6
Peterson, Arthur L., 119n
Peterson, Donald O., 92
Pitkin, Hanna F., 76n, 85n
Platform, 2, 5–6; candidates' role, 123–24, 133–35; committee chairman, 124–25, 129–30; committee composition, 115, 140, 179; committee role, 126–28; content, 110–14, 116; drafting, 114–20, 179; elimination proposal, 132–33; hearings, 115–18, 122, 179; minority report, 100–101, 118–19, 131, 178; national committee proposal, 135–37; and party out of power, 5, 6, 121–22, 128–29; and President, 116–19, 129–31; and presidential candidate, 123–24, 140; reform of, 130–32; significance of, 109–14; staff role, 128–29, 140; studies of, 110–14
Polling of delegation, 150; origin, 13; reform proposals, 105–6, 179. *See also* Unit rule
Polsby, Nelson, 173, 175
Pomper, Gerald, 110–14, 116
Population: in apportionment formula, 20–23, 26, 30–31, 33–36, 38–40, 42, 45, 47–48, 178; delegate selection, 70
President: midterm convention proposal, 138; and national convention, 5; platform role, 116–19, 129–31; in platform reform proposals, 136
Presidential candidate: candidate platform proposal, 133–35; caucus system, 1; front-runner, 13; midterm convention proposal, 138; minor, 8, 71, 83–84, 97; nominating rules, 101–2
Press. *See* News media
Primaries, presidential, 14, 52–53, 55–58, 73; national primary proposal, 172–77

Procedural rules, 5–6; Democratic, 98–106; reform recommendations, 178–79; Republican, 12, 98–103
Progressive party, 7, 18
Proxy voting: ban on, 69, 72; in delegate selection, 55, 69
Puerto Rico, 22, 88

Radio, 157–58
Ranney, Austin, 2n, 7n, 124, 173–74
Rauh, Joseph L., Jr., 66
Rayburn, Sam, 82, 97
Reagan, Ronald, 122
Republican Coordinating Committee, 121–22
Republican National Committee: and apportionment system, 18, 20–21; convention reforms, 11–12; convention responsibility, 88, 99; and delegate selection, 63, 69, 72; procedural rules, 99
Republican National Convention: *1912*, 17–18, 22–23, 35; *1952*, 11, 63–64, 87, 149; *1956*, 87, 116–17; *1960*, 87, 119, 126; *1964*, 2, 7, 11–12, 87, 95, 107, 110, 142, 144, 154; *1968*, 59–60, 69, 87; *1972*, 23, 26
Republican party: apportionment system, 19–27, 34–35, 43–45, 47, 50; convention rules, 11–12; delegate selection, 11–12, 53, 62–64, 69, 71–75, 92; factions in, 69; political style, 11; procedural rules, 97–103, 105
Ripon Society, and apportionment, 21–22, 50
Robert's Rules of Order, 99
Robinson, John P., 145n, 155n
Rockefeller, Nelson A., 120, 122–23, 126, 133, 155
Rocky Mountain states, 43, 45, 47–48
Roll call, 150–51; reforms, 102–3, 105, 179
Romney, George, 152
Roosevelt, Theodore, 17–18, 62
Roper, Burns W., 143n, 146n
Roper poll, 143, 145
Roseboom, Eugene H., 18n
Rossiter, Clinton, 11
Rothchild, John, 153n
Rourke, Francis E., 153
Rules. *See* Procedural rules
Rules committee, 6

San Francisco, 2
Scammon, Richard M., 60n

Schlesinger, Arthur M., Jr., 4, 5*n*

Scranton, William, 129, 152

Security, in national convention: Democratic, 93–94, 166; Republican, 12. *See also* Behavior

Senator, and apportionment formulas, 21, 23, 29, 34

Sevareid, Eric, 155

Shattuck, Frances M., 117*n*

Site selection, 149–50, 164–65

Smiley, D. V., 132*n*

Soule, John W., 4*n*, 59, 85*n*

South: *1912* Republican convention, 17–18, 34; black franchise, 75; bonus votes, 20; credentials contests, 62–67; delegate loyalty, 78; Republicanism in, 26–27; unit rule, 39; voting strength of, 43, 45, 47–48

South Carolina, 29

Sovereignty. *See* State sovereignty

Spanish-speaking citizens. *See* Minorities

Staff, national convention, 5–6, 82, 86, 97, 162–64

State chairman, 55, 82–84, 92, 140

State sovereignty, and apportionment formulas, 21–23, 31, 35

States, large vs. small, 27, 31, 33, 35, 38–41, 43, 45, 47, 136

States' Rights party, 29, 64

Stephenson, William A. F., 58*n*

Stevenson, Adlai, 29, 94*n*, 123–24, 143, 150

Sundquist, James L., 110

Survey Research Center, 144–45

Taft-Hartley Act, 111–12

Taft, Robert A., 11, 62–63, 124, 133, 155

Taft, William Howard, 17–18, 21, 62

Television: convention reporting, 14, 95–96, 143–44, 149–52, 156–57, 165–71; and national primary proposal, 176

Temple, David, 58*n*

Territories, apportionment systems, 22, 29–30. *See also* Canal Zone; Guam; Puerto Rico; Virgin Islands

Texas, 64

Thomson, Charles A. H., 117*n*, 143*n*, 144*n*

Tillett, Paul, 58*n*, 86*n*, 109, 119*n*

Truman, Harry S, 29, 57, 117, 126

Unit rule, 38; in delegate selection, 55–

56; Democratic ban, 9–10, 39, 68–69, 73, 84, 104–5; reform proposal, 179; Republican use, 39, 71. *See also* Polling of delegation

United Press International (UPI), 158

U.S. Court of Appeals, 18–20

U.S. District Court, 19–20

U.S. House of Representatives, 98–100

U.S. Supreme Court, 18, 20, 79–80

Vanocur, Sander, 151

Vice President: in candidate platform proposal, 134–35; nomination proposals, 103–4

Vietnam war, 28, 117–18, 122, 124, 127, 132–33, 150, 165–66

Virgin Islands: apportionment formulas for, 22, 29; delegation size, 88

Vote apportionment. *See* Apportionment system

Voting, in national convention, 91, 100, 105–6. *See also* Polling of delegation; Roll call; Unit rule

Wallace, George, 20, 23, 27, 58*n*, 64, 78, 109

Walsh, Robert, 134*n*

Waltzer, Herbert, 163*n*

Wattenberg, Ben J., 60*n*

Wesberry v. Sanders (1964), 20*n*

Whale, John, 157*n*

White, F. Clifton, 107*n*

White, Theodore H., 2*n*, 107*n*, 119*n*, 120*n*, 122*n*, 170

Whiteside, Thomas, 163*n*, 166*n*, 170*n*

Wildavsky, Aaron B., 86*n*, 173, 175

Wilkins, Roy, 169

Willkie, Wendell, 109

Wisconsin, 53, 125, 174

Women: in apportionment formulas, 37; as committee delegates, 90; in delegate selection, 59–61, 70, 74–76. *See also* Minorities

Write-in votes, 58

Youth: in apportionment formulas, 37–38; as committee delegates, 90–91; in delegate selection, 59–61, 70

Zeidenstein, Harvey, 134*n*